Darling Kayla ...

We visited this gallery

enjoyed the beautiful photographic works,

taken in and around Australia, by a

local artist, Ken Duncan.

He's included some lovely inspirational

quotes as well. Enjoy...

Love to you, from me.

x x x

ENJOY THE JOURNEY

INSPIRATIONAL *Joy*

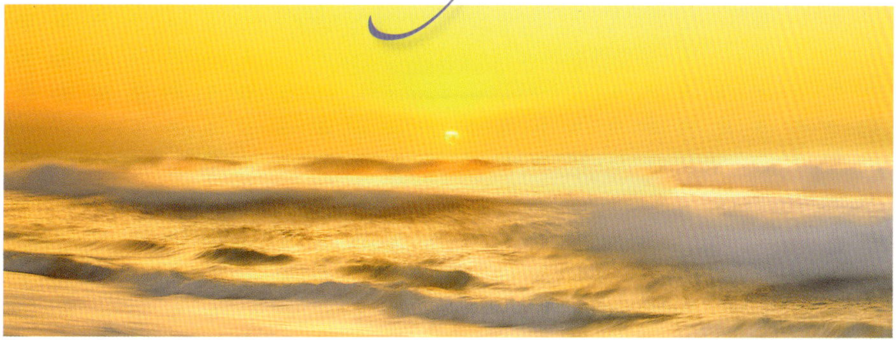

AUSTRALIAN PHOTOGRAPHS BY KEN DUNCAN

PANOGRAPHS®
PUBLISHING PTY LTD

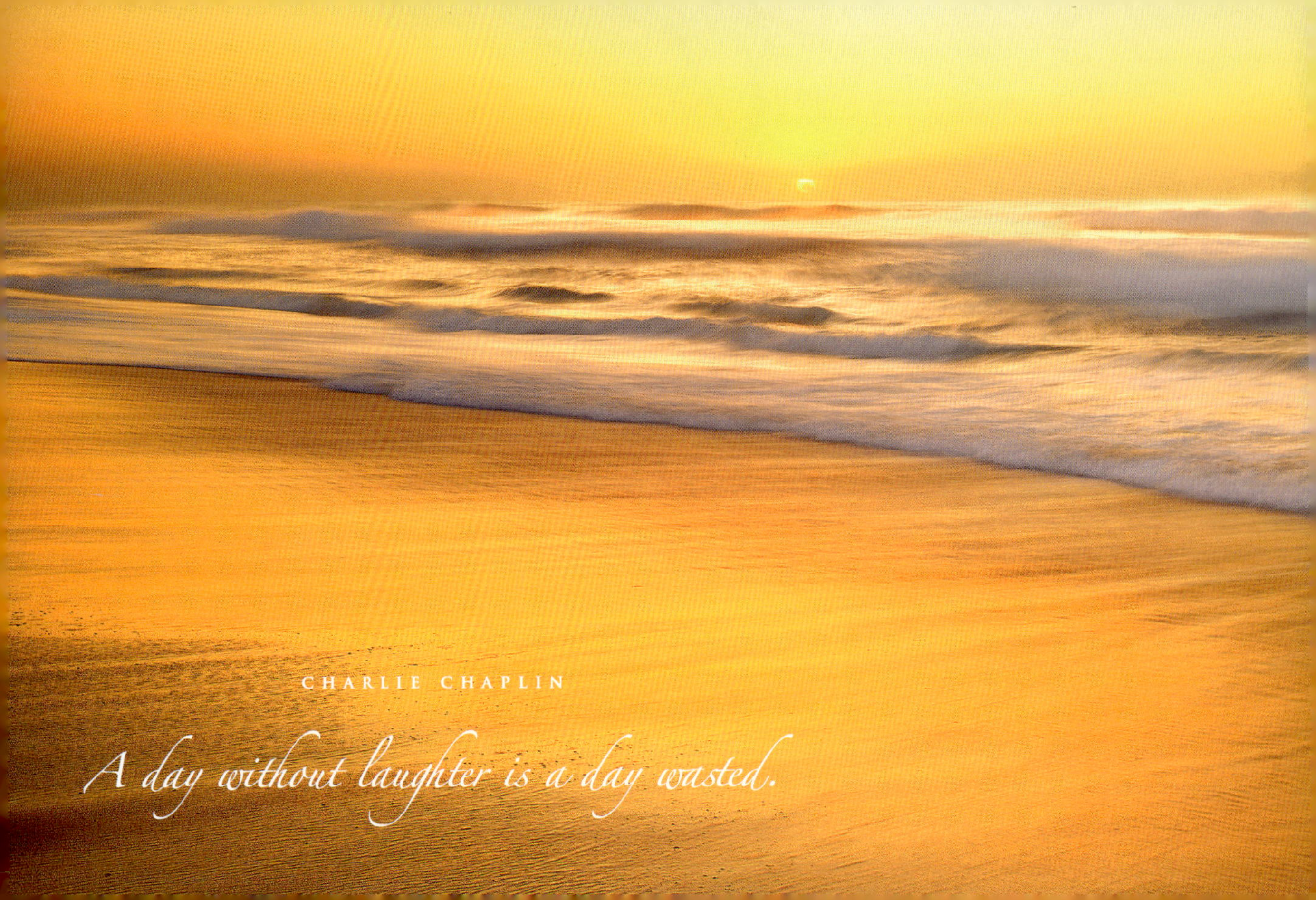
CHARLIE CHAPLIN
A day without laughter is a day wasted.

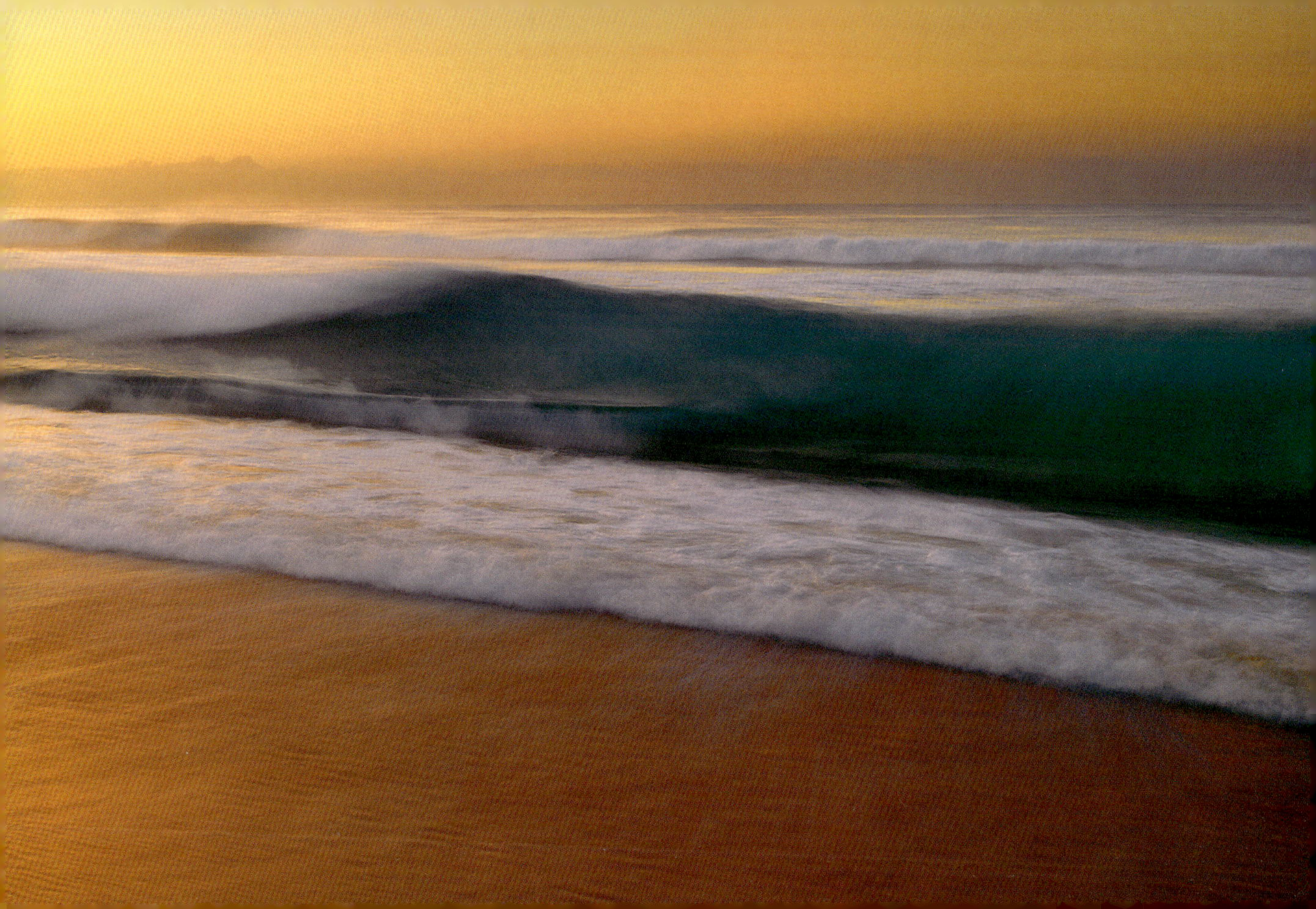

Some cause happiness wherever they go; others whenever they go. OSCAR WILDE

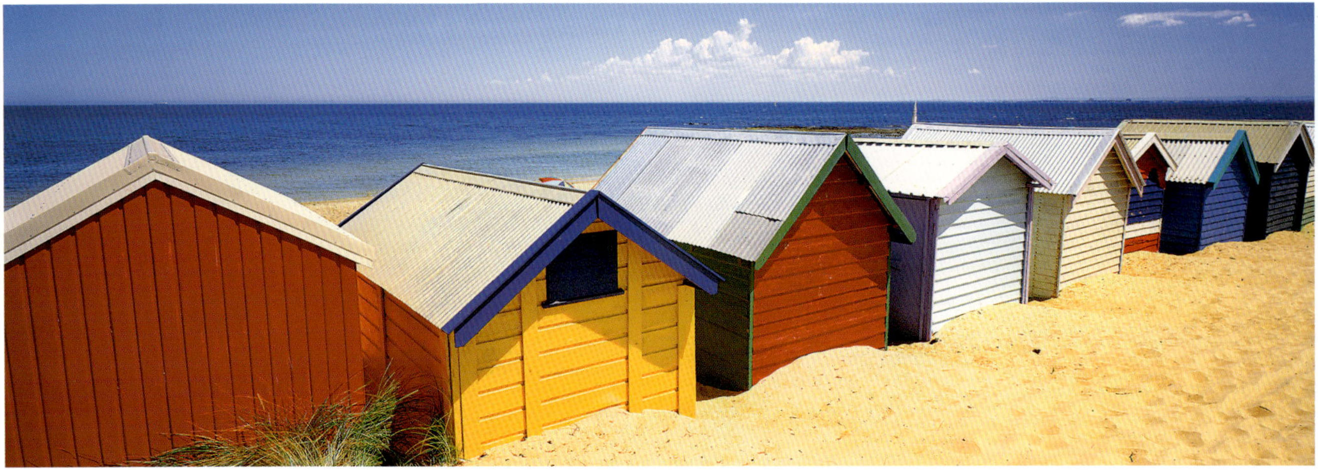

FRONT COVER *Glory of Spring, Wynyard, Tas*
PREVIOUS PAGE *New Beginnings, Terrigal Beach, NSW*
THIS PAGE *Brighton Beach Huts, Vic*

— INTRODUCTION —

According to the popular adage, laughter is the best medicine. Even science now confirms that a joyful heart brings healing to the whole body. But in a busy world which is changing so rapidly, it can be difficult to push aside the pressures of life.

As you reflect upon the beauty of creation in these Australian photographs, I hope the inspired wisdom of the accompanying text will help lift you into an atmosphere of true joy – joy that remains, despite the circumstances of your life. Remember ... he who laughs, lasts.

Happiness is a perfume you cannot pour on others without getting a few drops on yourself.

Serenity, Mullengandra, NSW

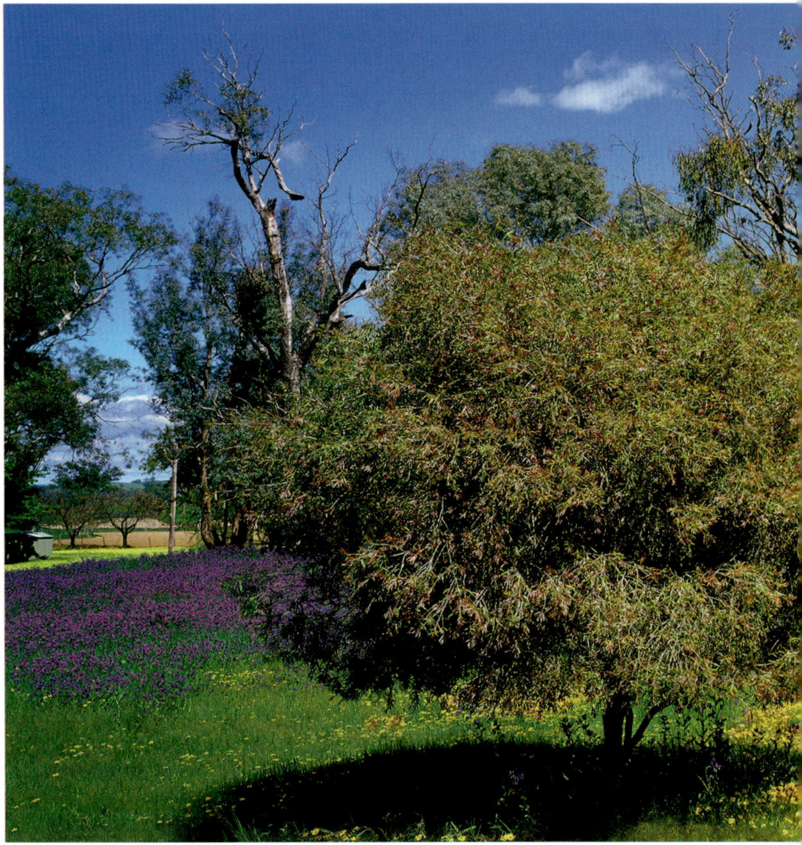

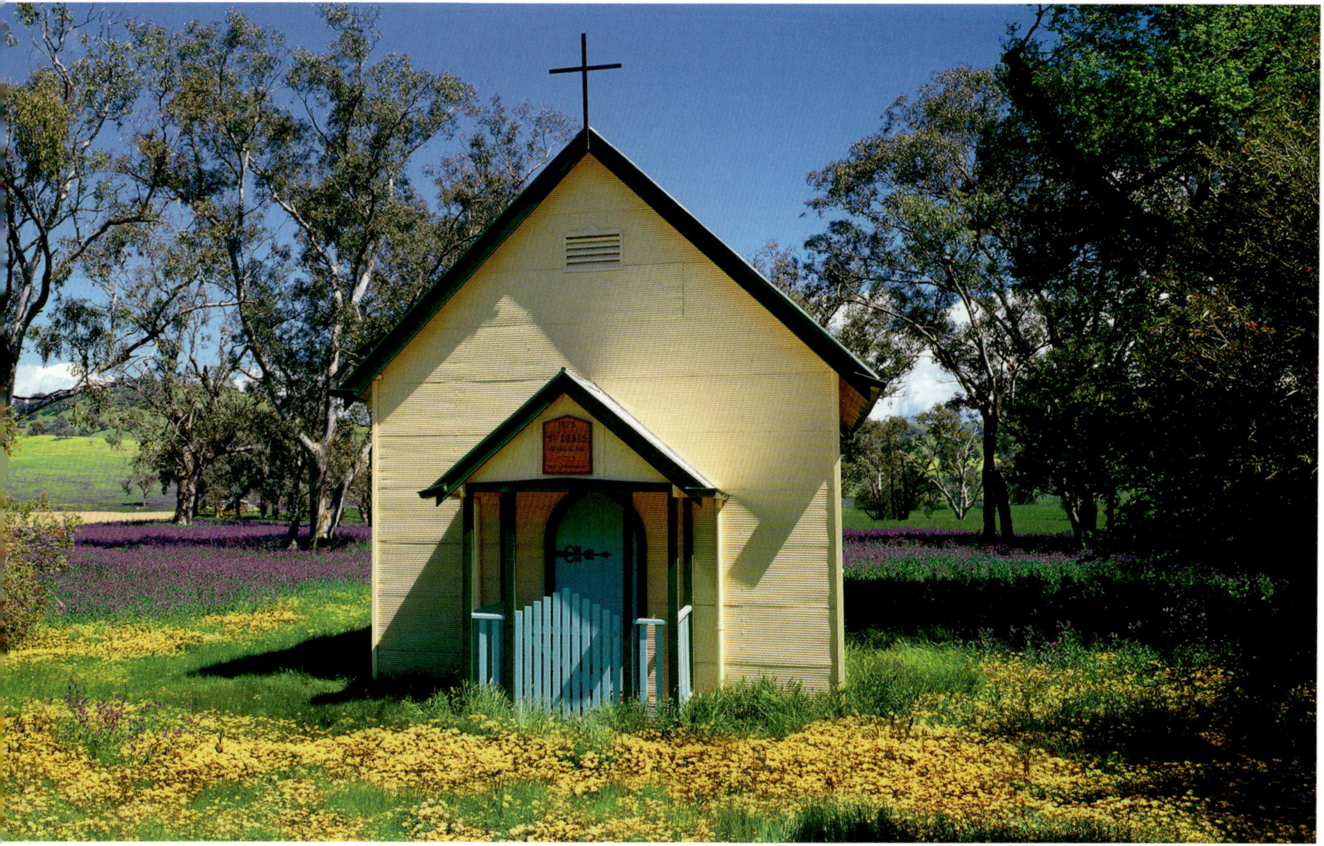
ANGLICAN

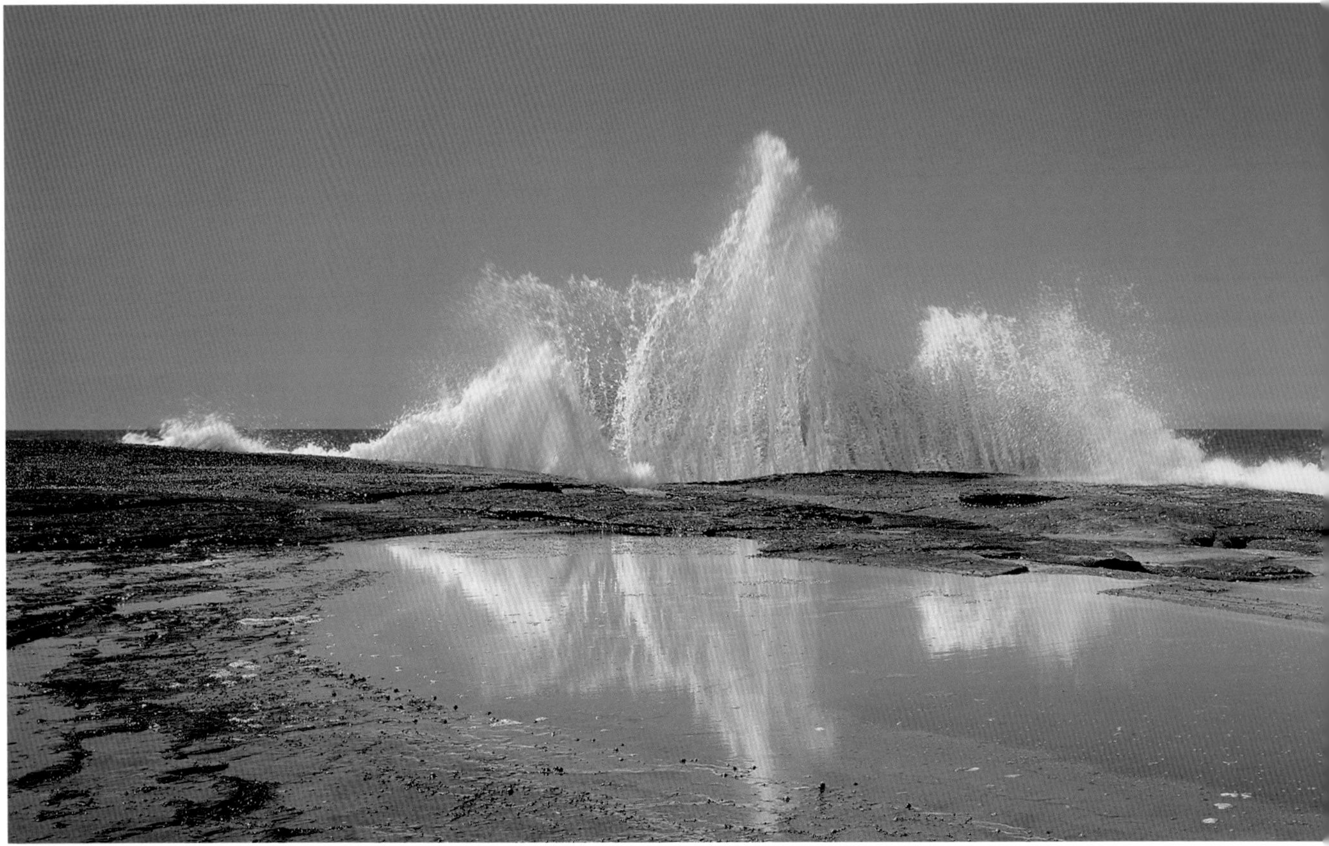

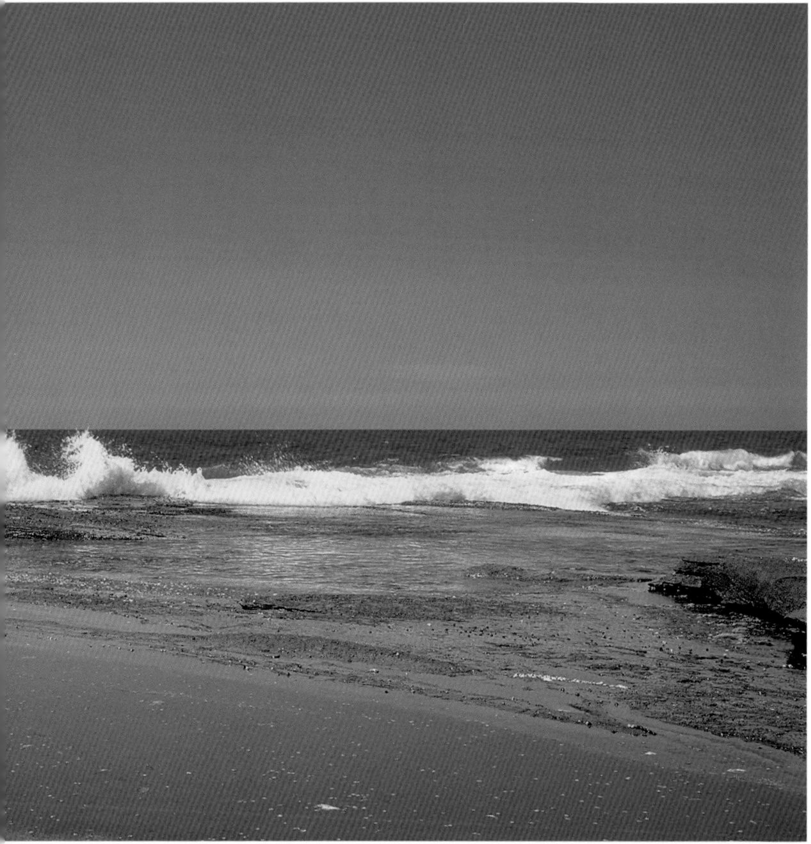

Singing Joy to the world
all the boys and girls, now
Joy to the fishes in the deep blue sea,
Joy to you and me.

THIS PAGE
Ocean Symphony, Terrigal, NSW

FOLLOWING PAGES
Bell Gorge Falls, The Kimberley, WA

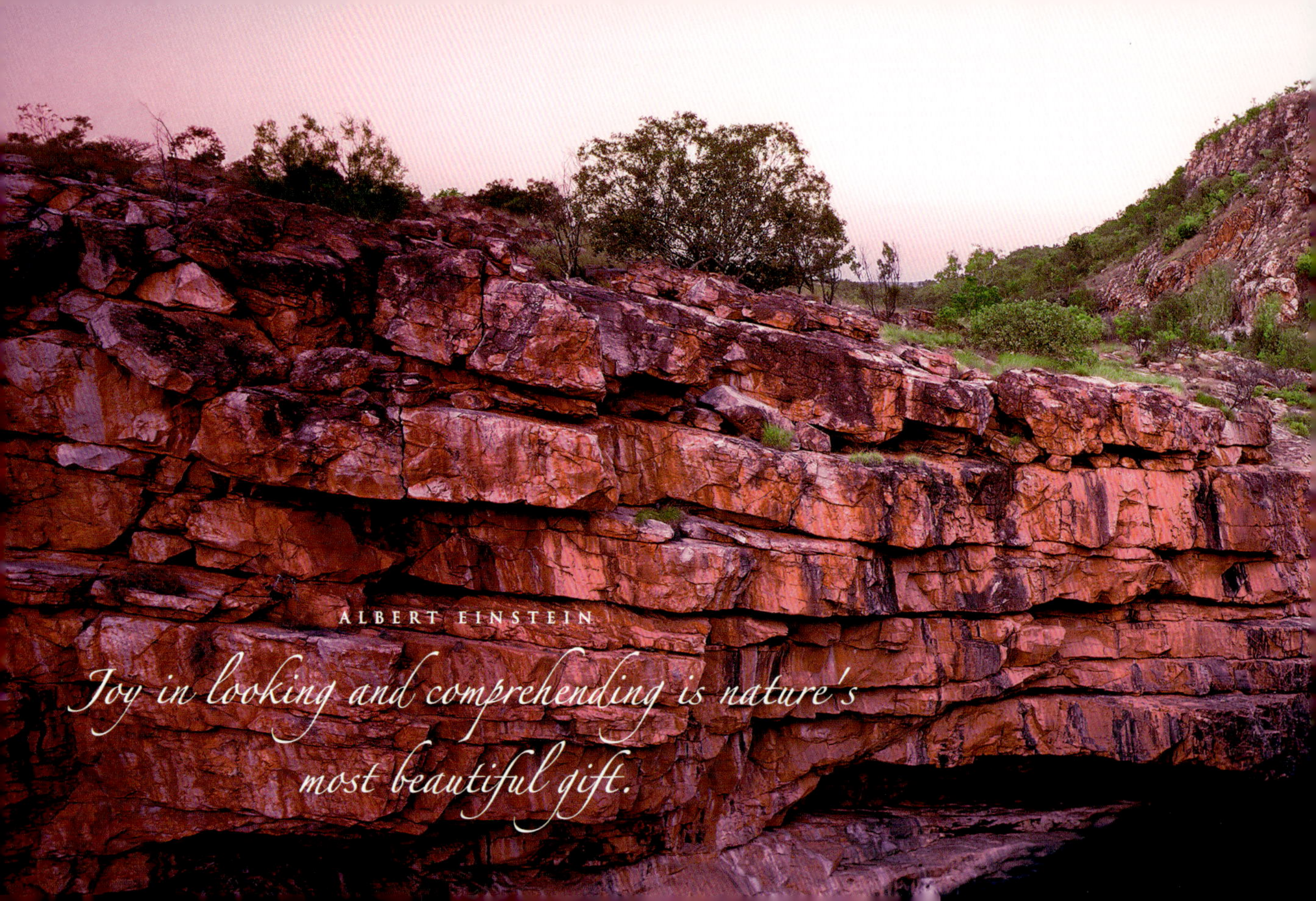

ALBERT EINSTEIN

Joy in looking and comprehending is nature's most beautiful gift.

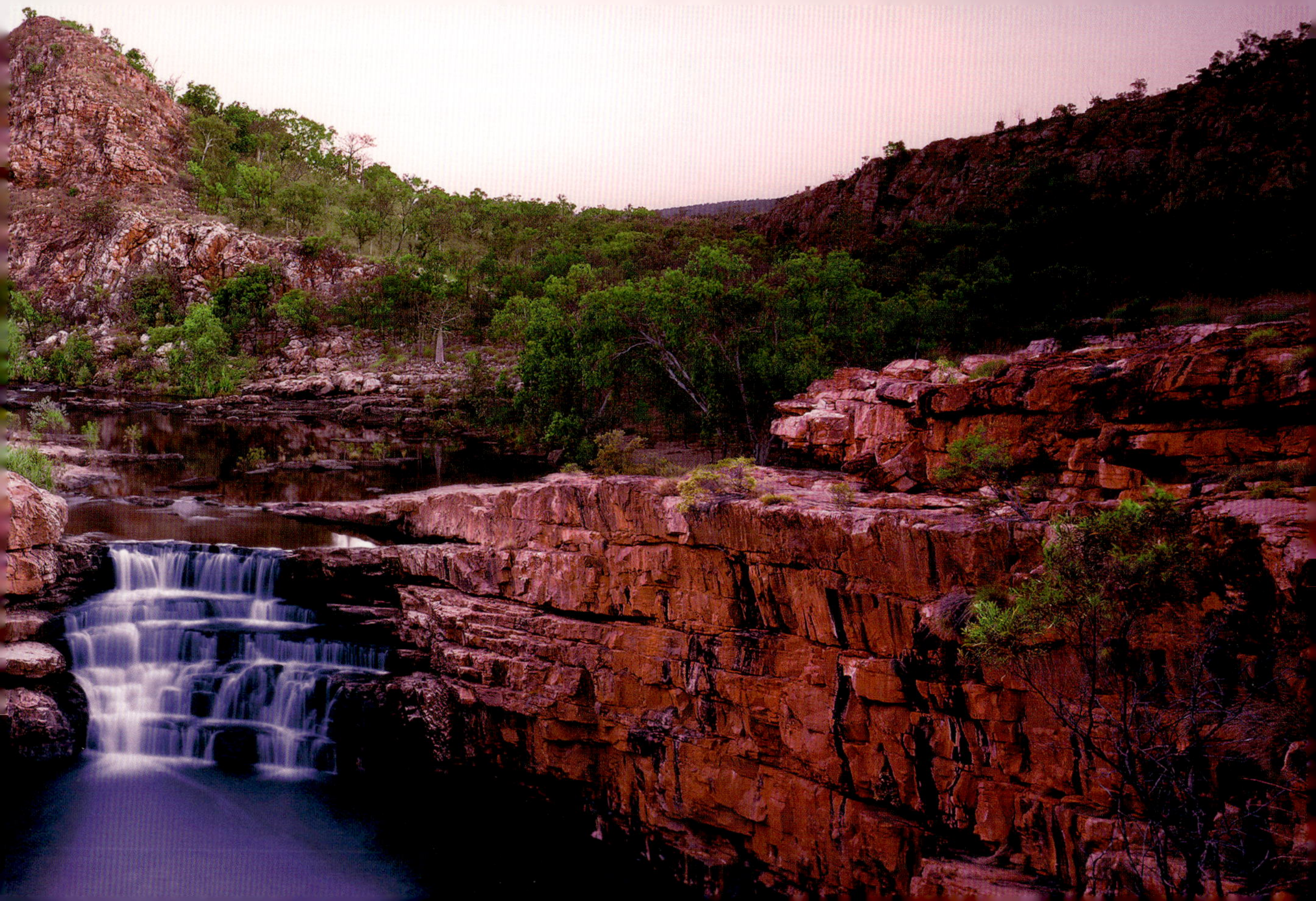

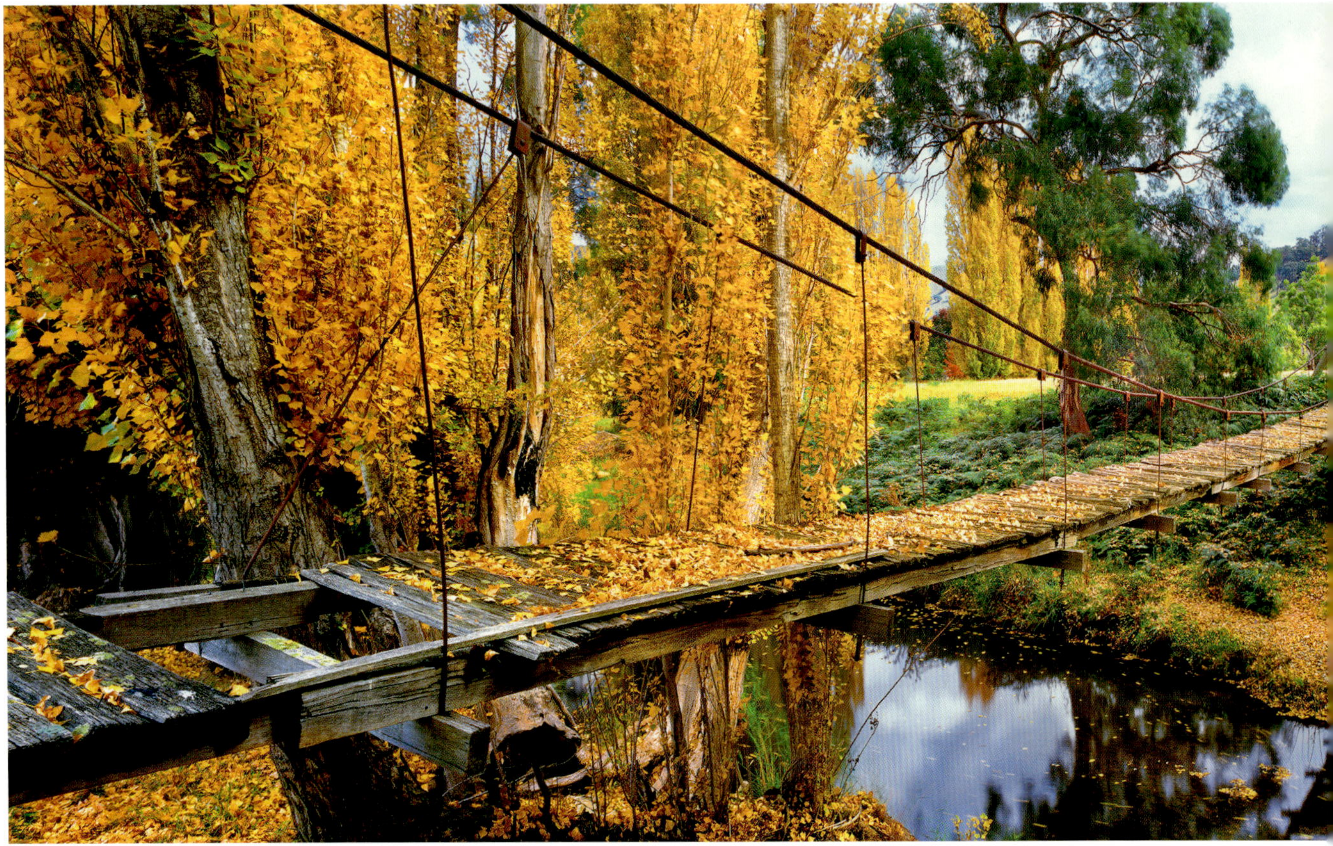

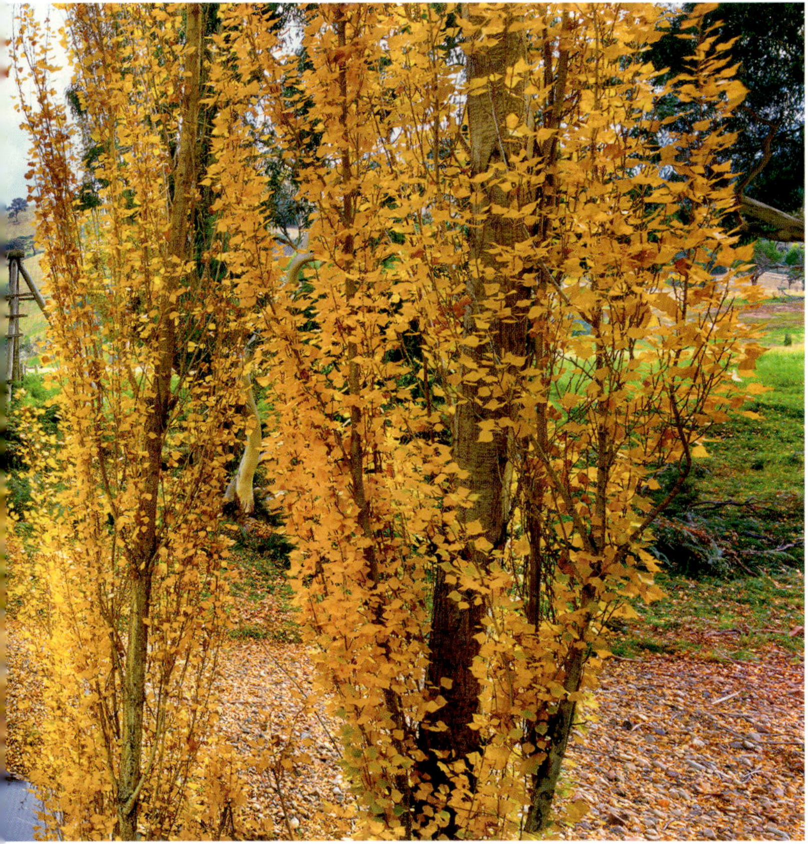

Do not put off till tomorrow
what can be enjoyed today.

The Crossing, Swifts Creek, Vic

ANON

The seed is Hope,
the flower is Joy.

THIS PAGE
Snowball Farm, Gundagai, NSW

FOLLOWING PAGES
Desert Showers, Uluru, NT

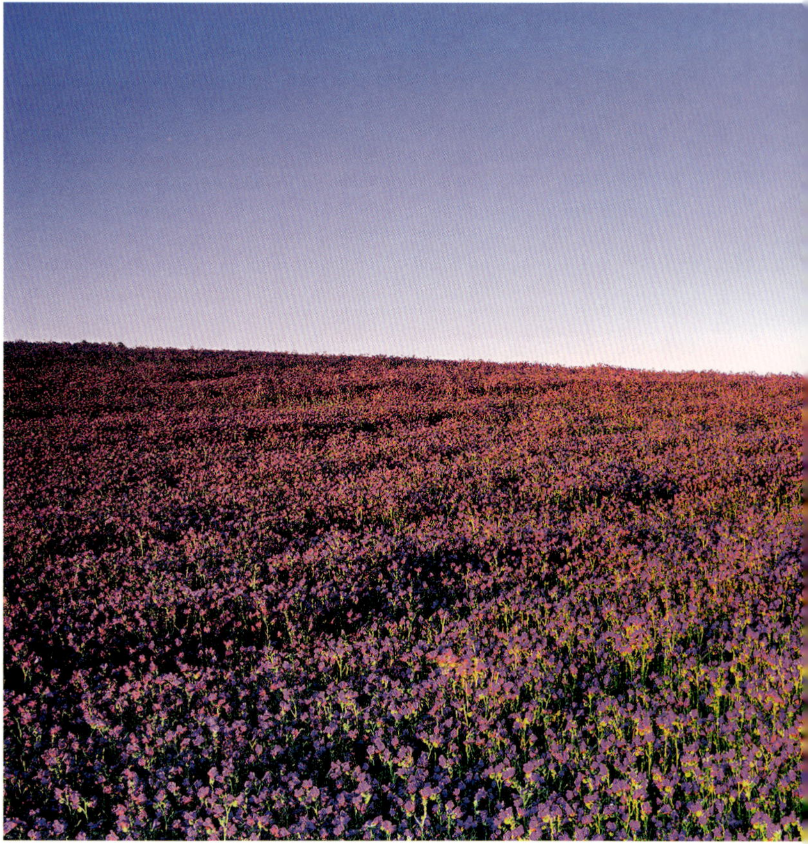

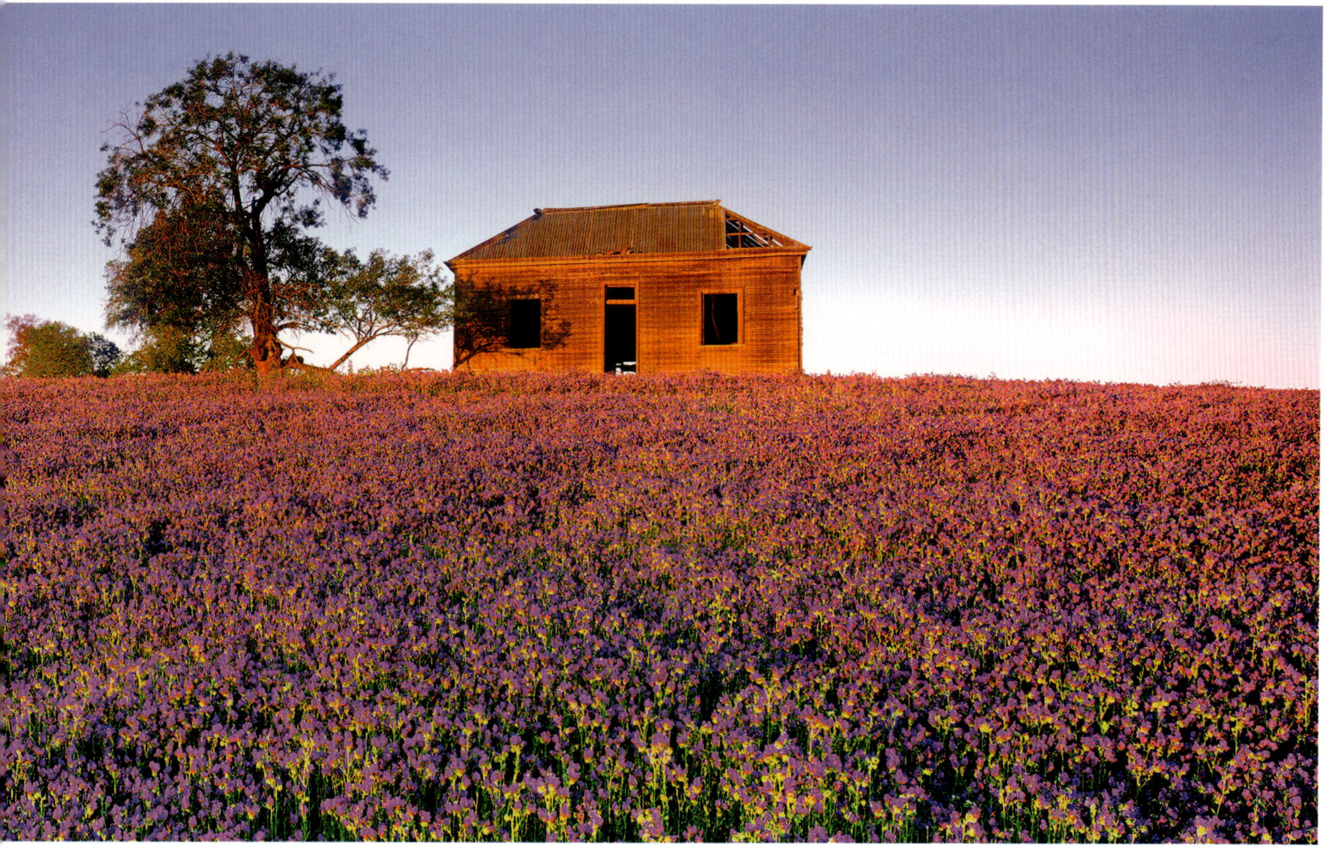

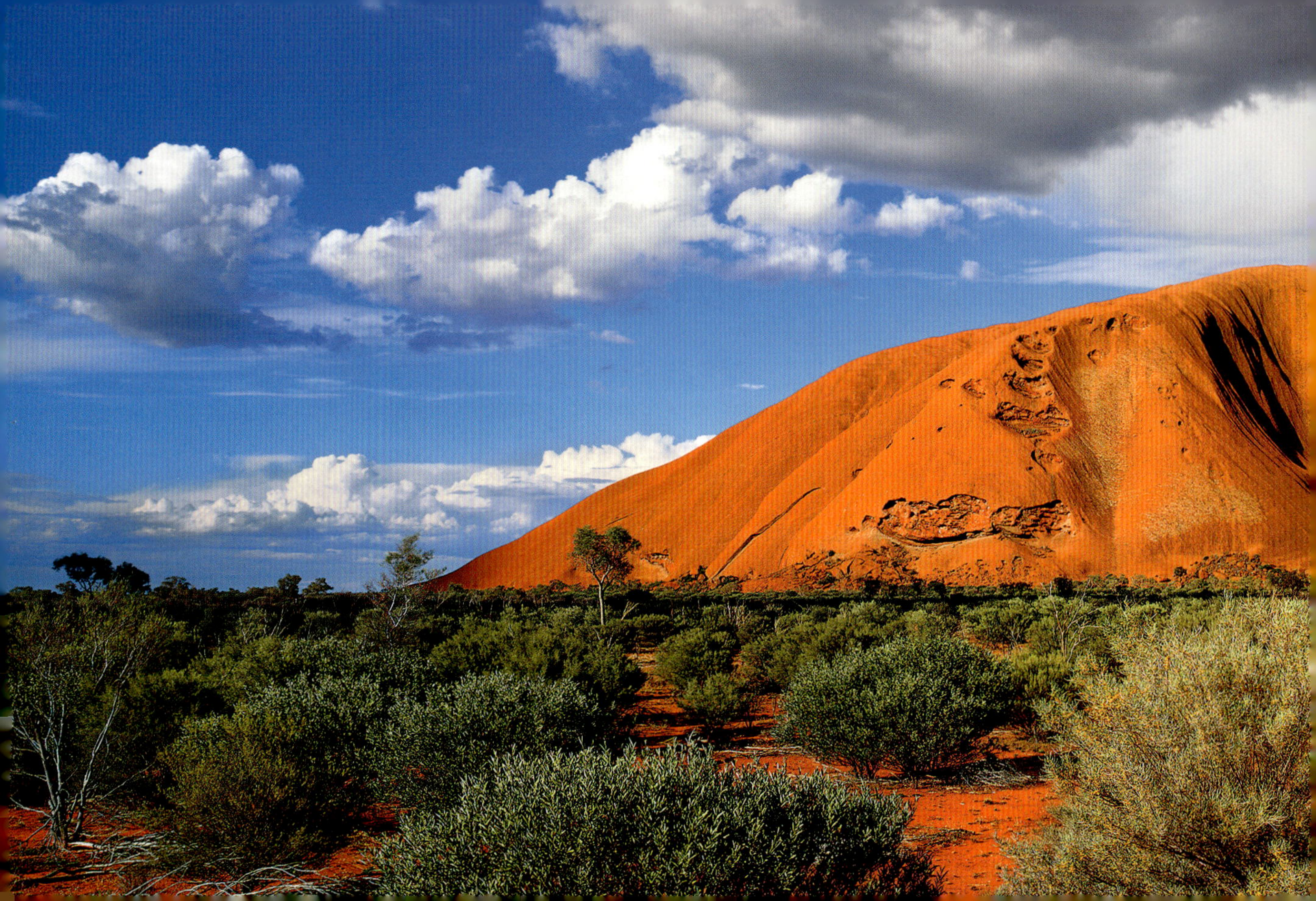

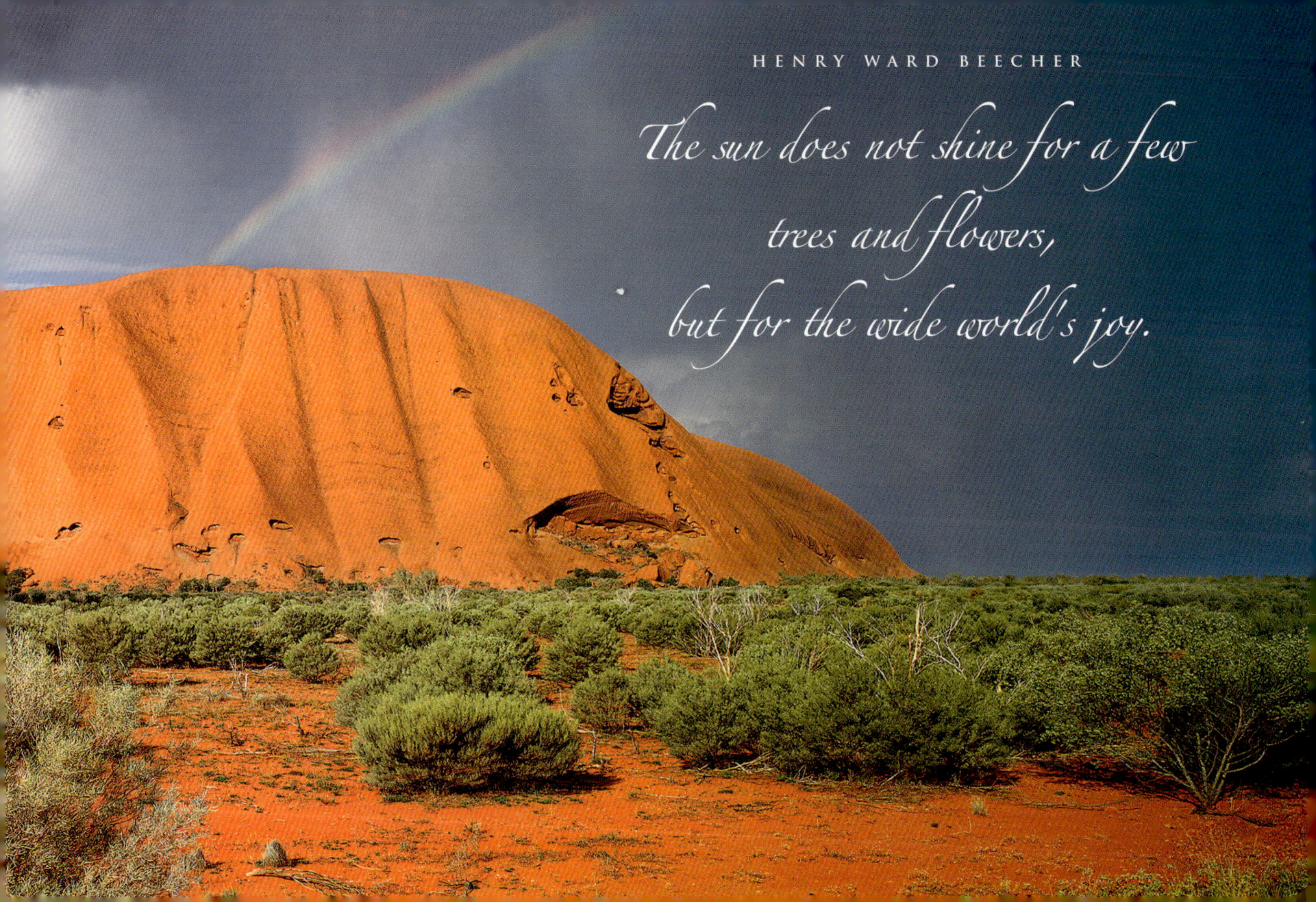

HENRY WARD BEECHER

The sun does not shine for a few
trees and flowers,
but for the wide world's joy.

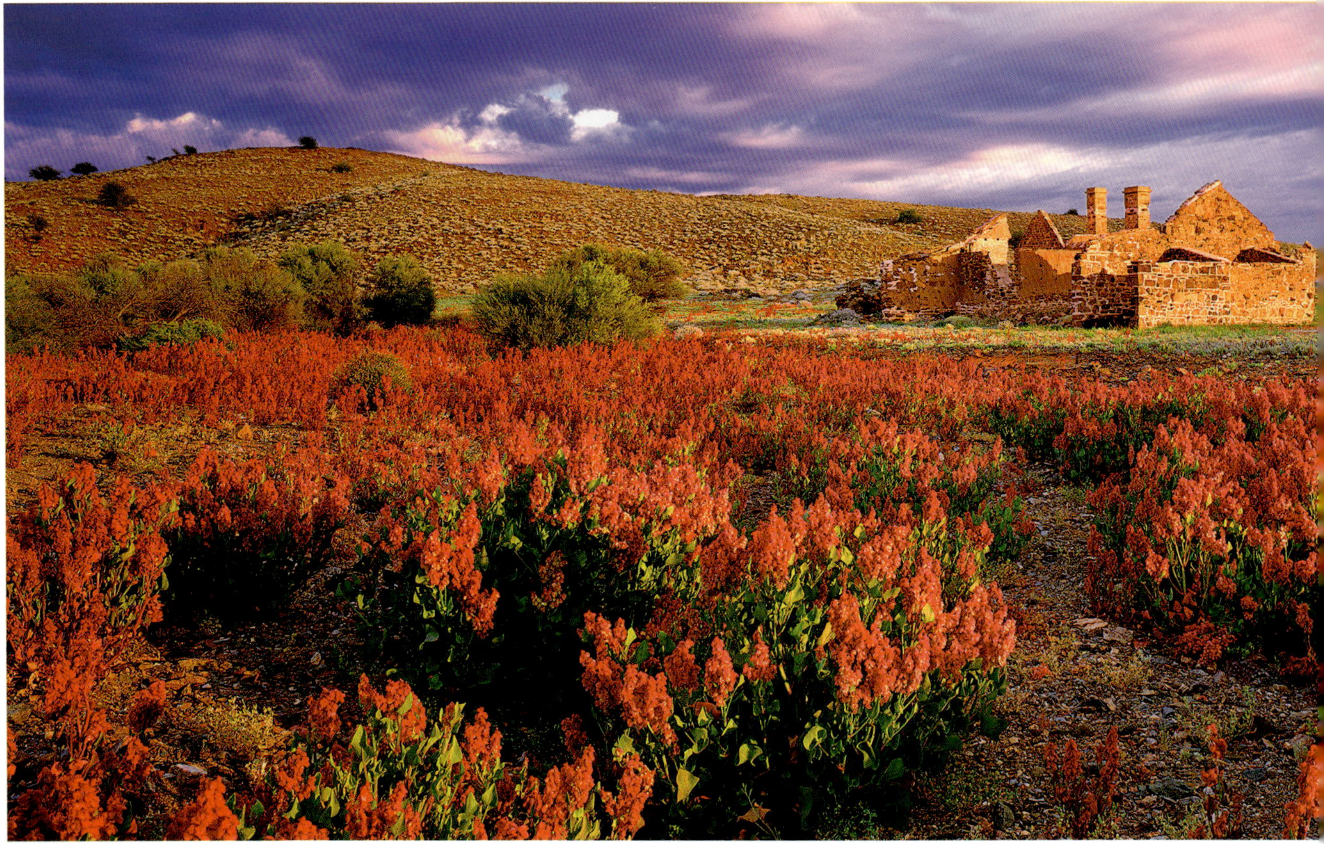

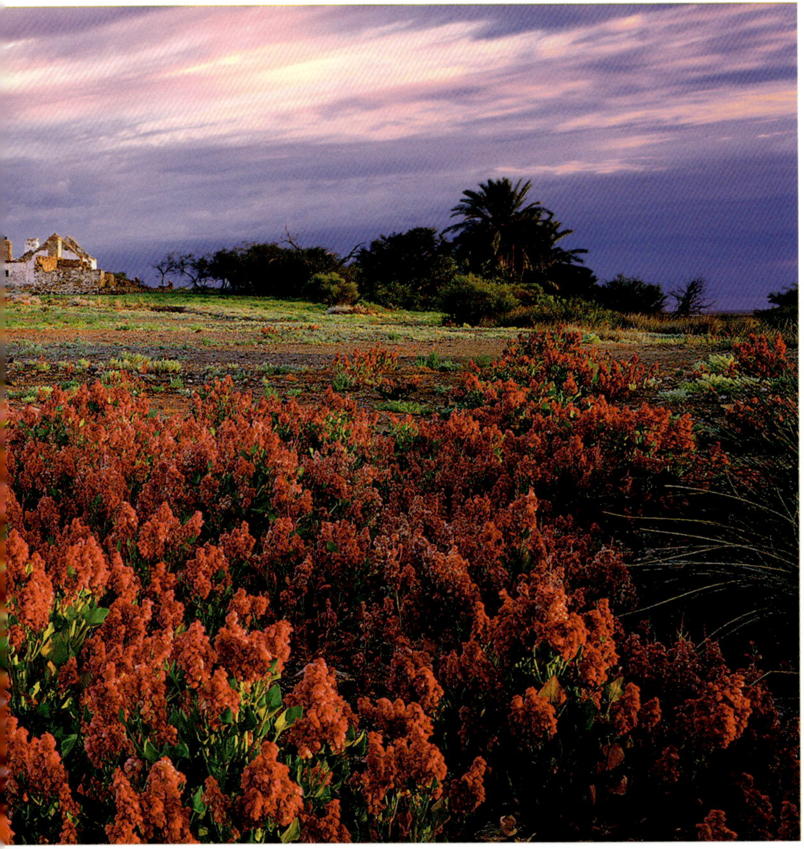

Happiness doesn't depend on any
external conditions,
it is governed by our mental attitude.

Peake Ruins, Oodnadatta, SA

PSALM 65:8

The whole earth is filled
with awe at your wonders;
where morning dawns,
where evening fades,
you call forth songs of joy.

THIS PAGE
River of Life, Ellery Creek, NT

FOLLOWING PAGES
Let there be Joy, Sunflowers, NSW

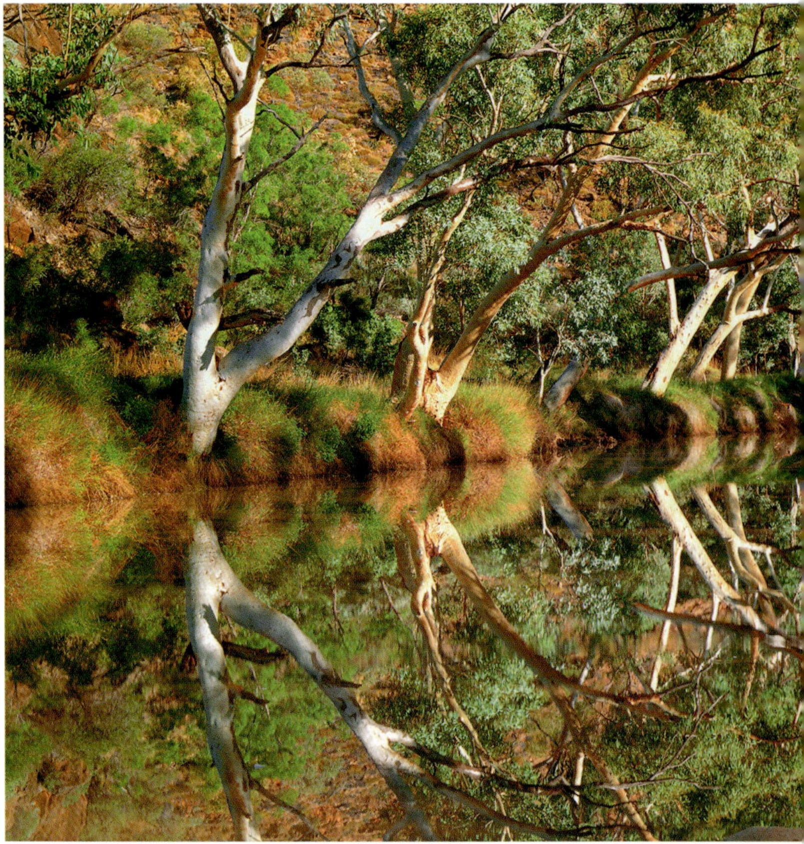

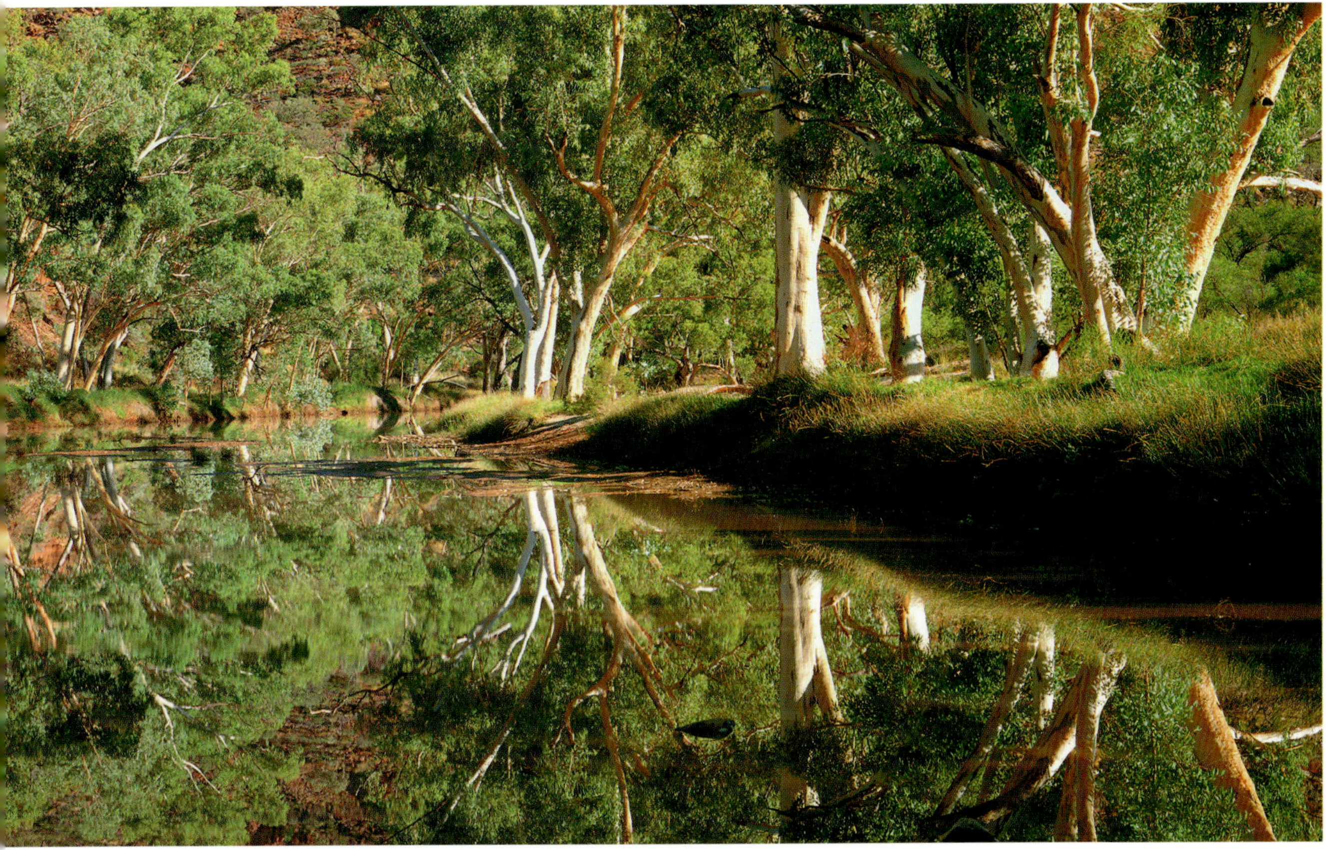

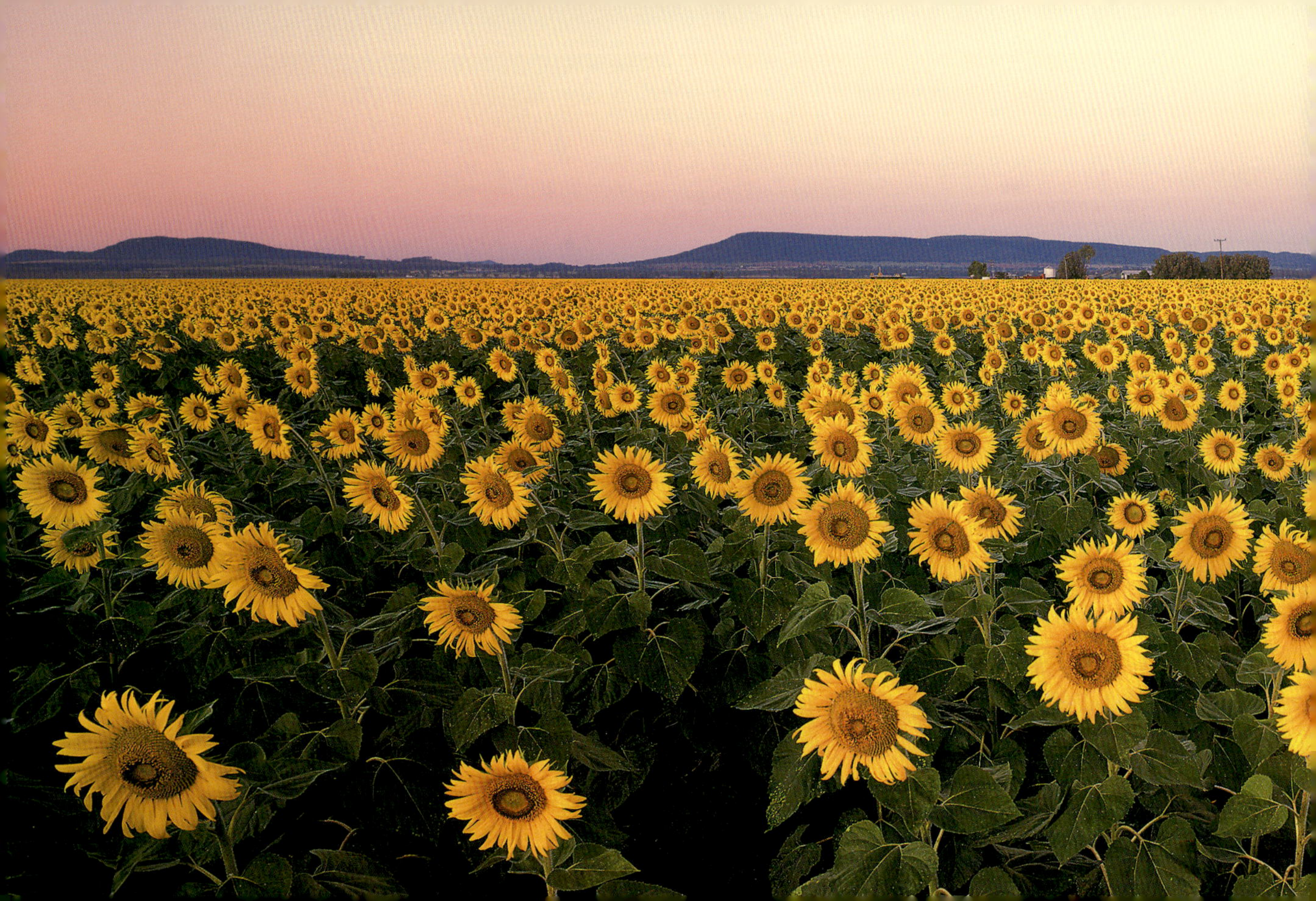

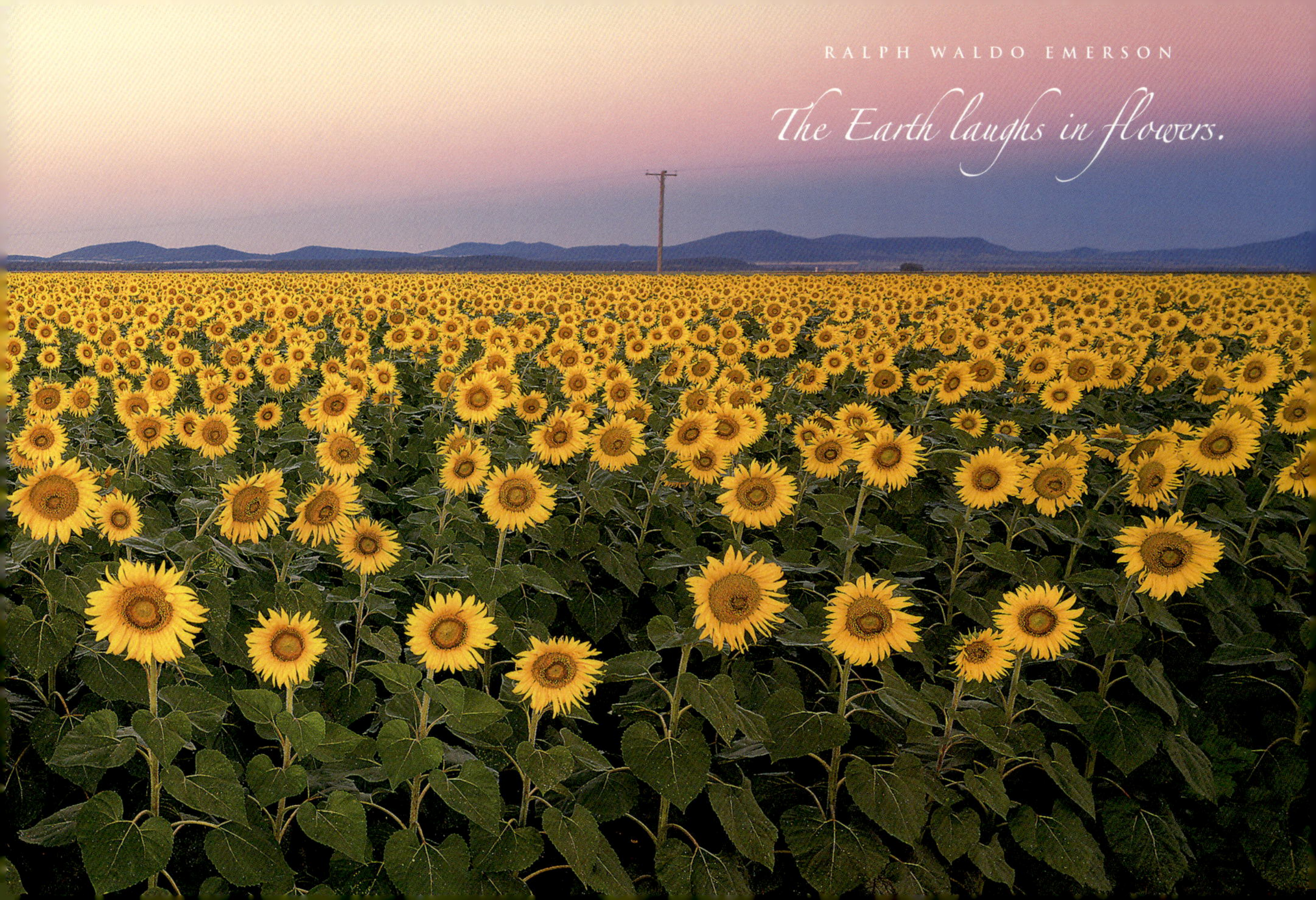
RALPH WALDO EMERSON
The Earth laughs in flowers.

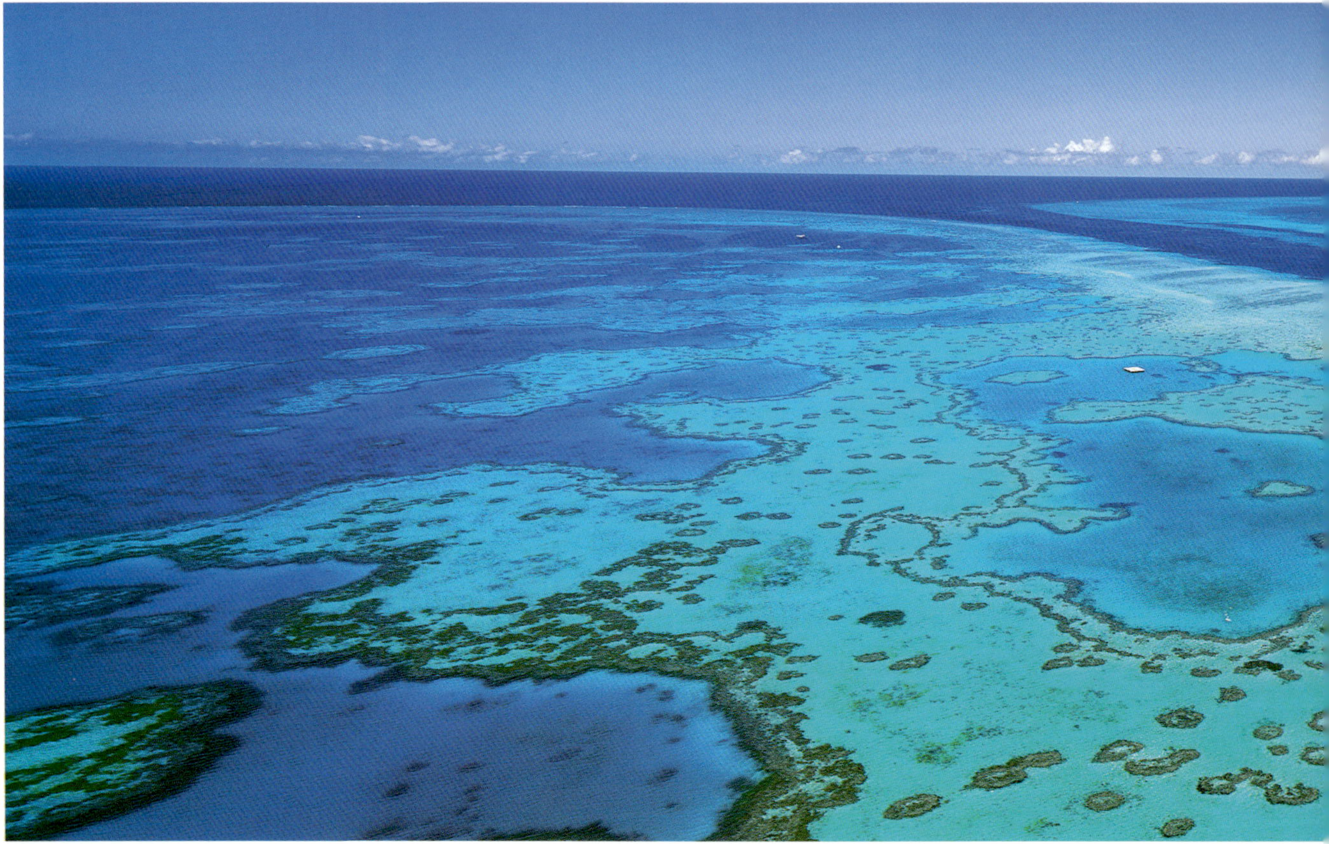

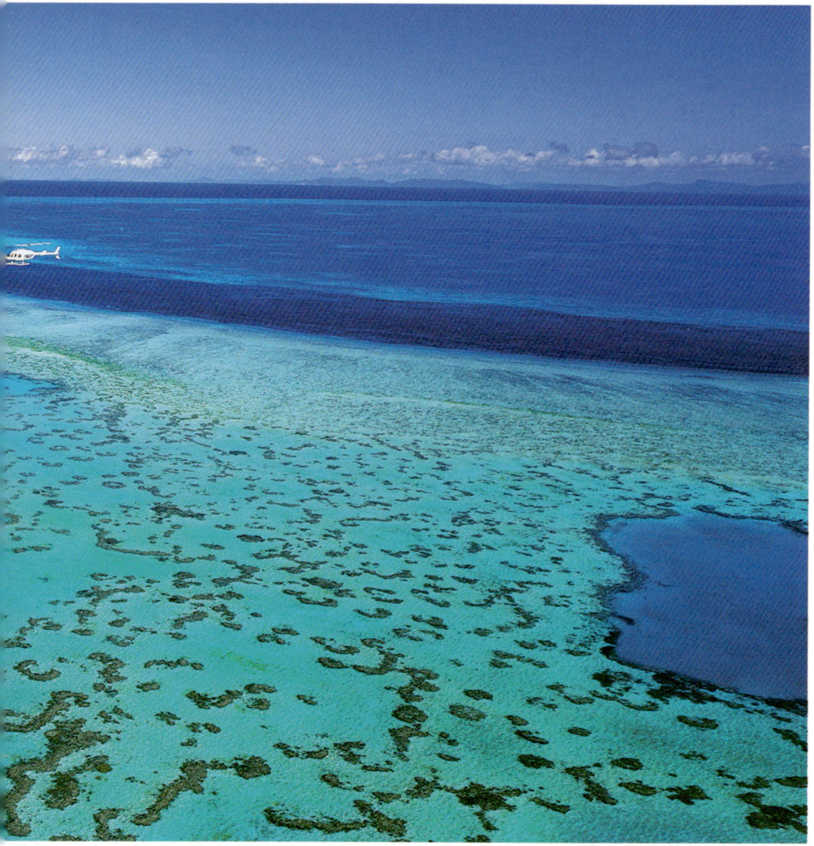

A thing of beauty is a joy forever:
its loveliness increases;
it will never pass into nothingness.

Heart Reef, Great Barrier Reef, Qld

Laughter is the joyous,
universal evergreen of life.

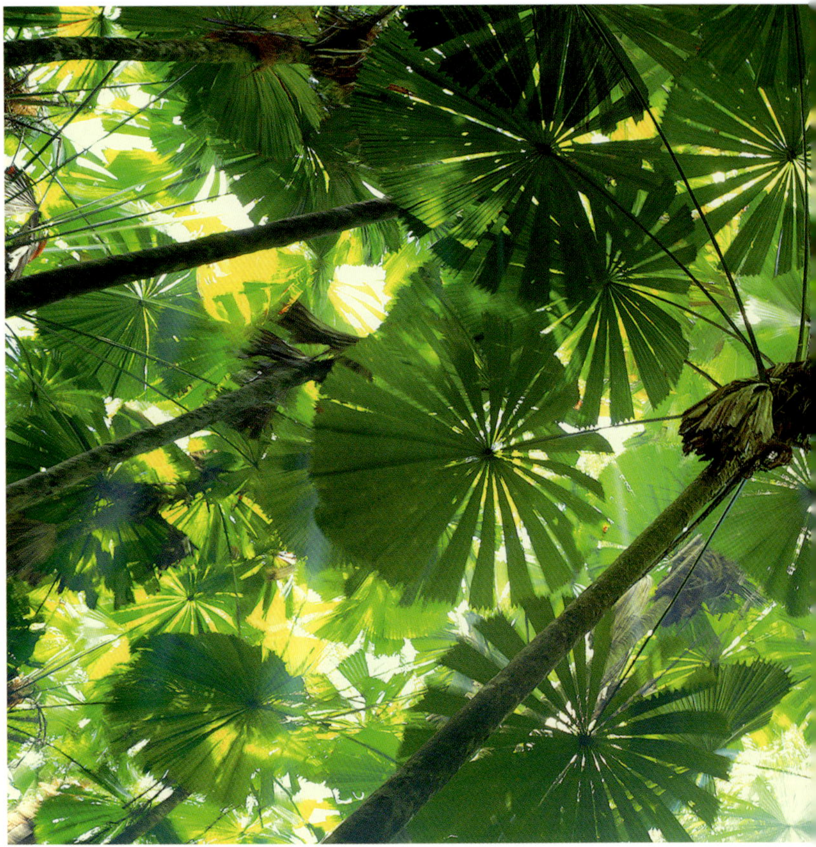

THIS PAGE
Fan Palms, Cape Tribulation, Qld

FOLLOWING PAGES
Hamersley Reflections, Hamersley Gorge, WA

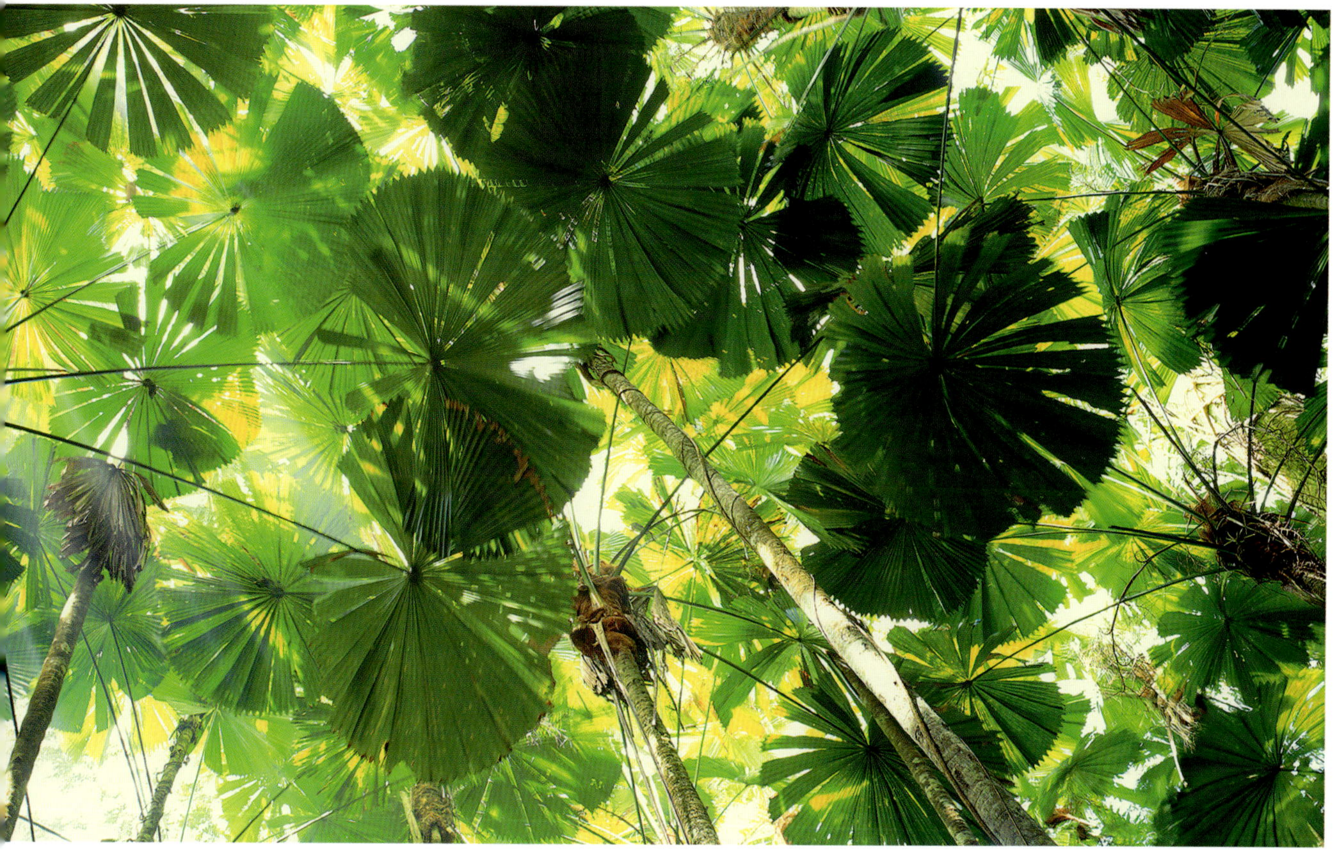

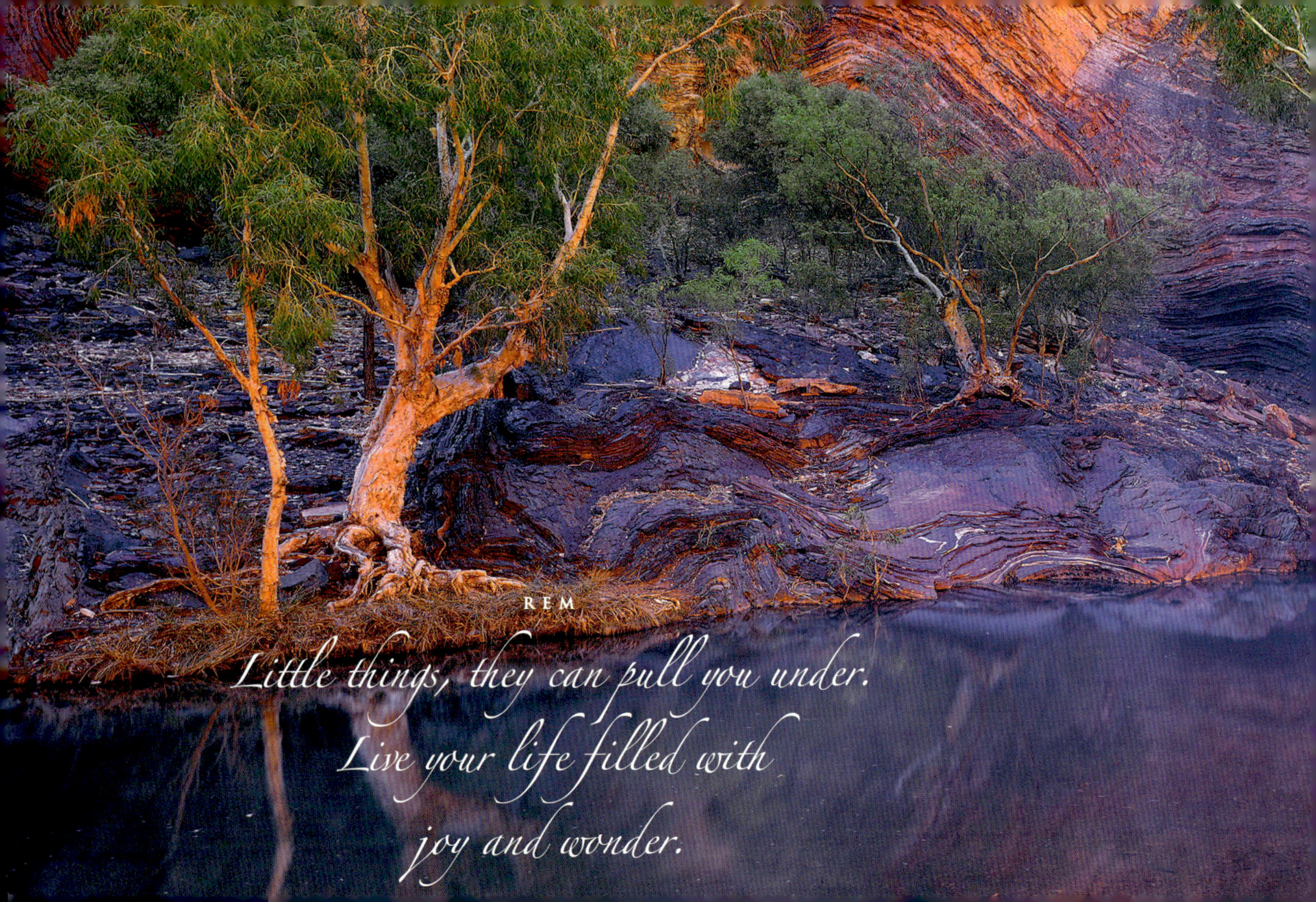
REM
Little things, they can pull you under.
Live your life filled with
joy and wonder.

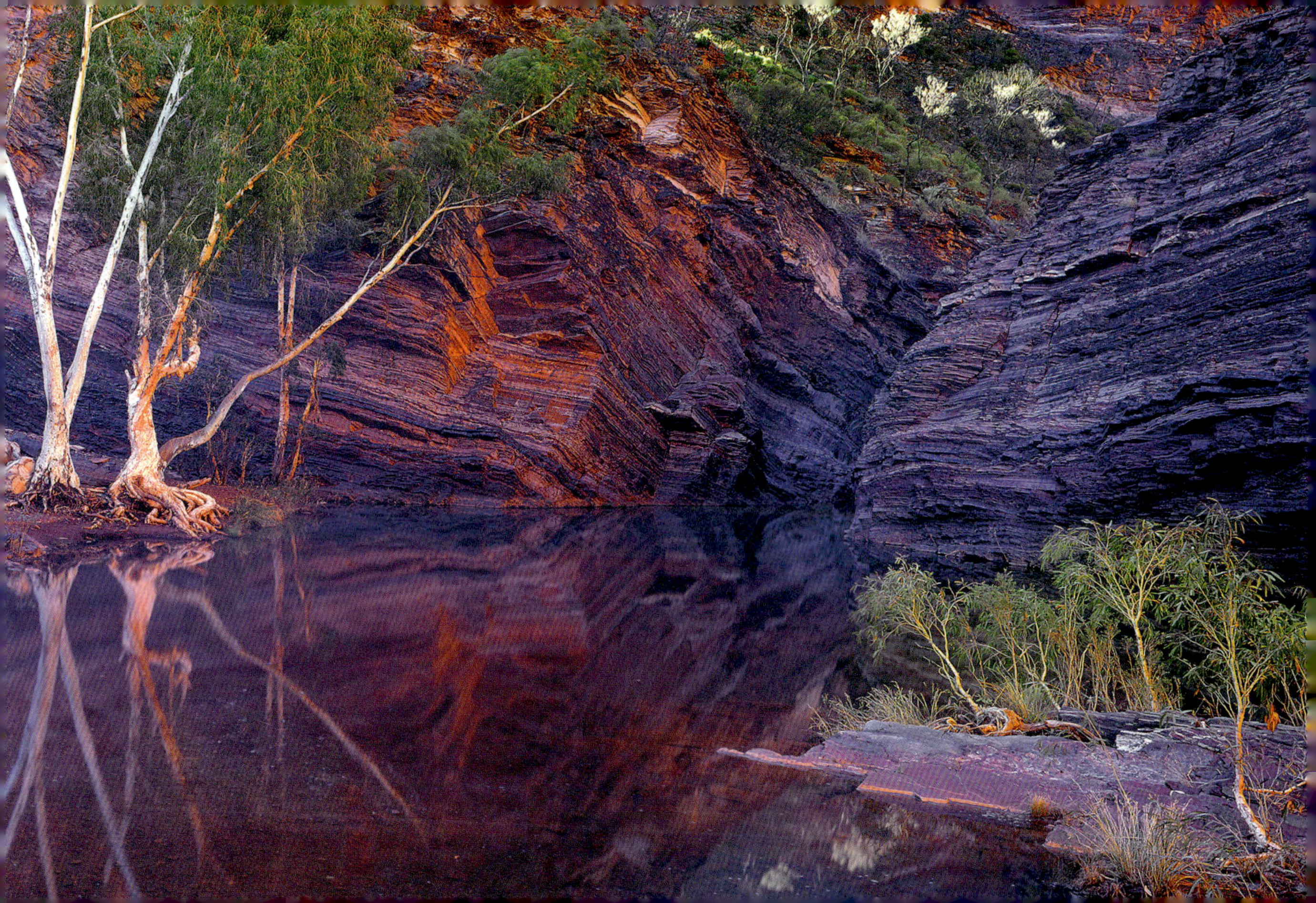

Time you enjoyed wasting,
was not wasted.

Paradise, Fantome Island, Qld

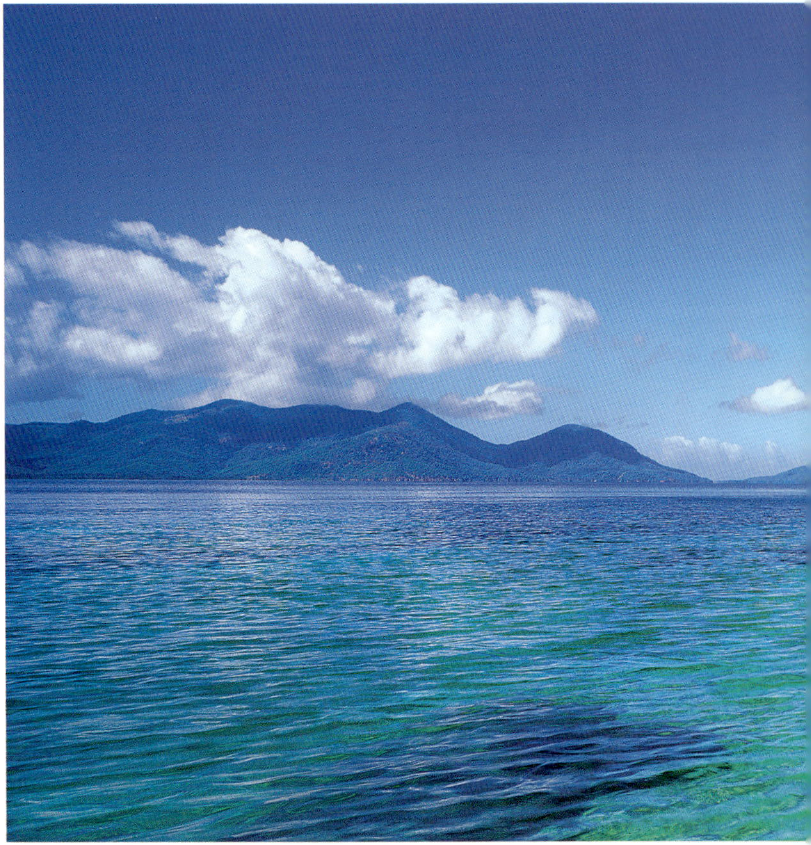

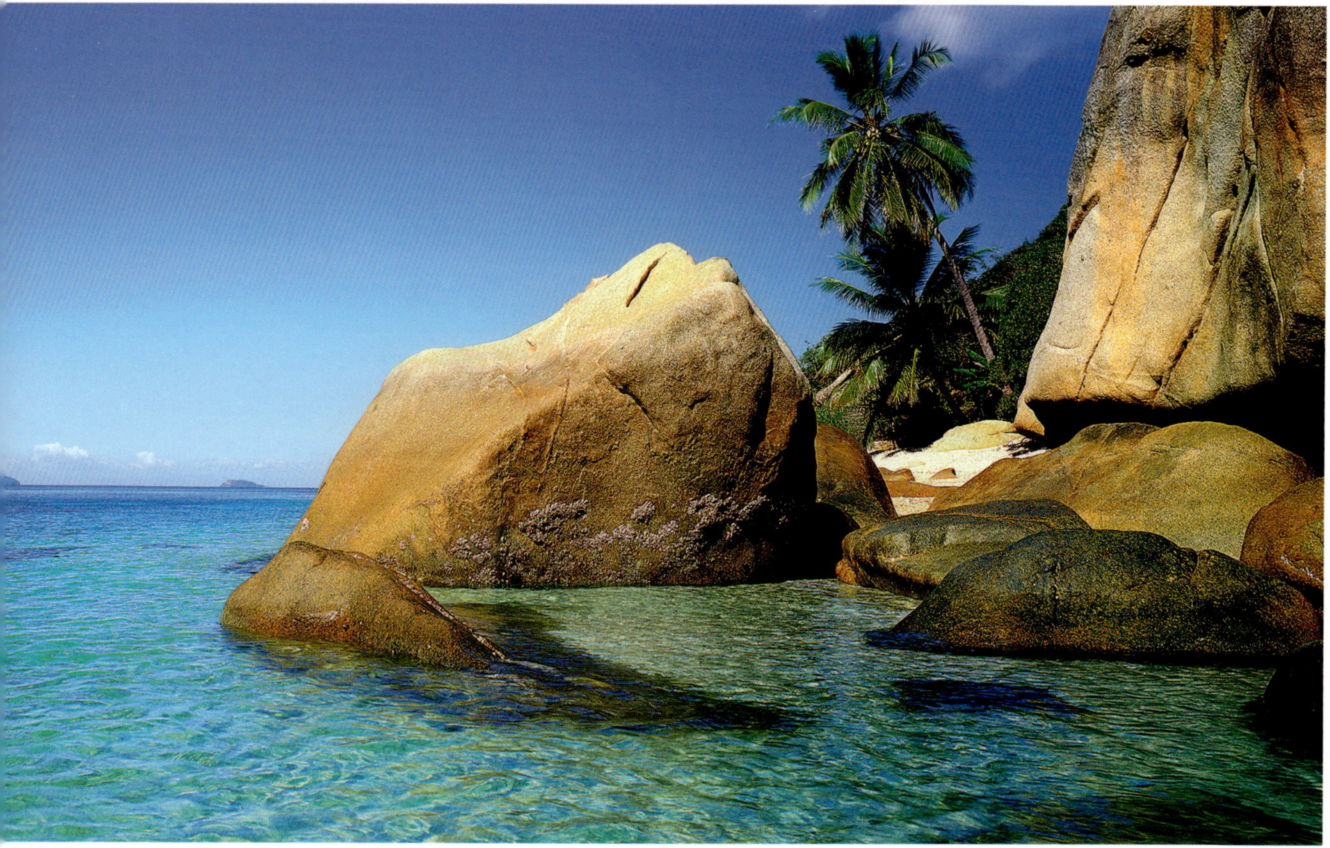

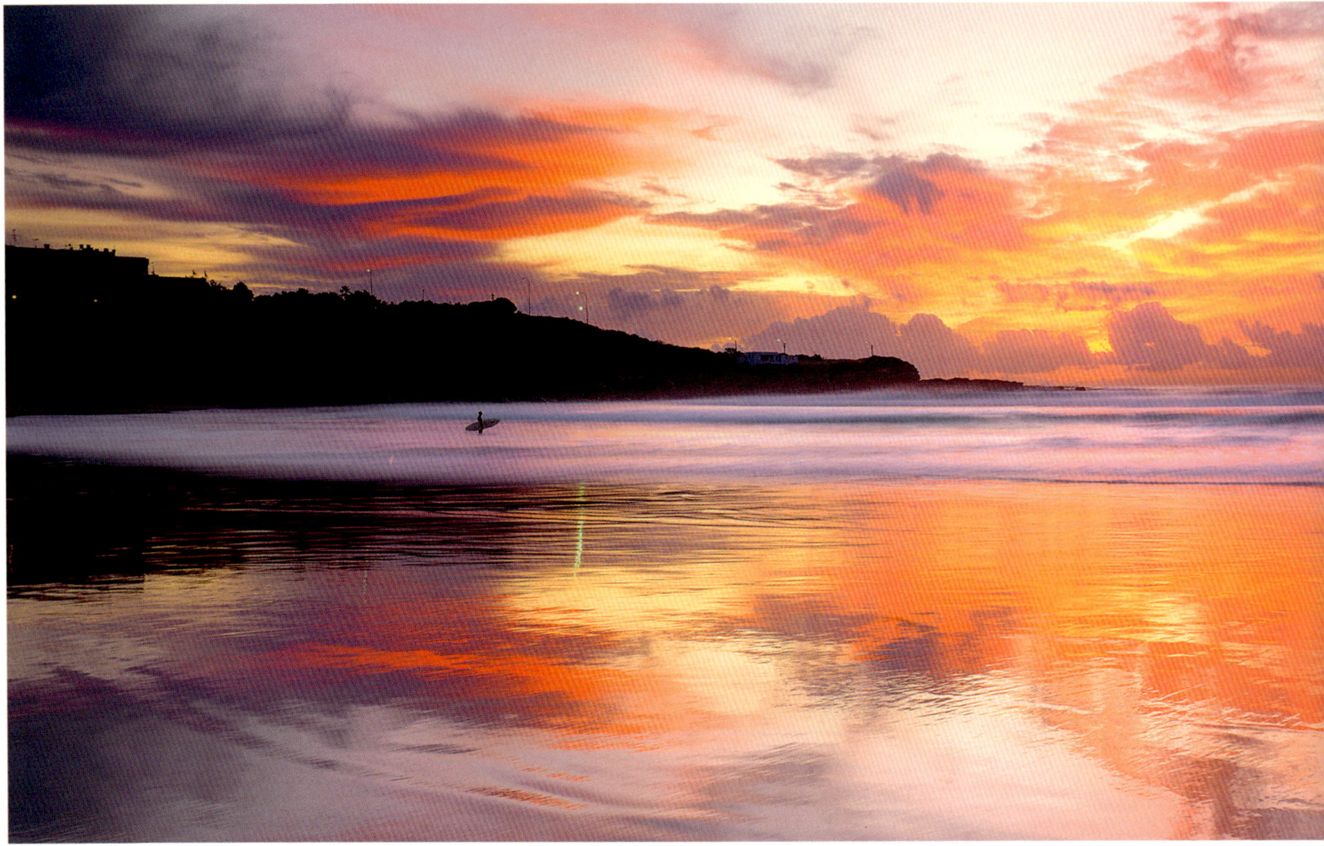

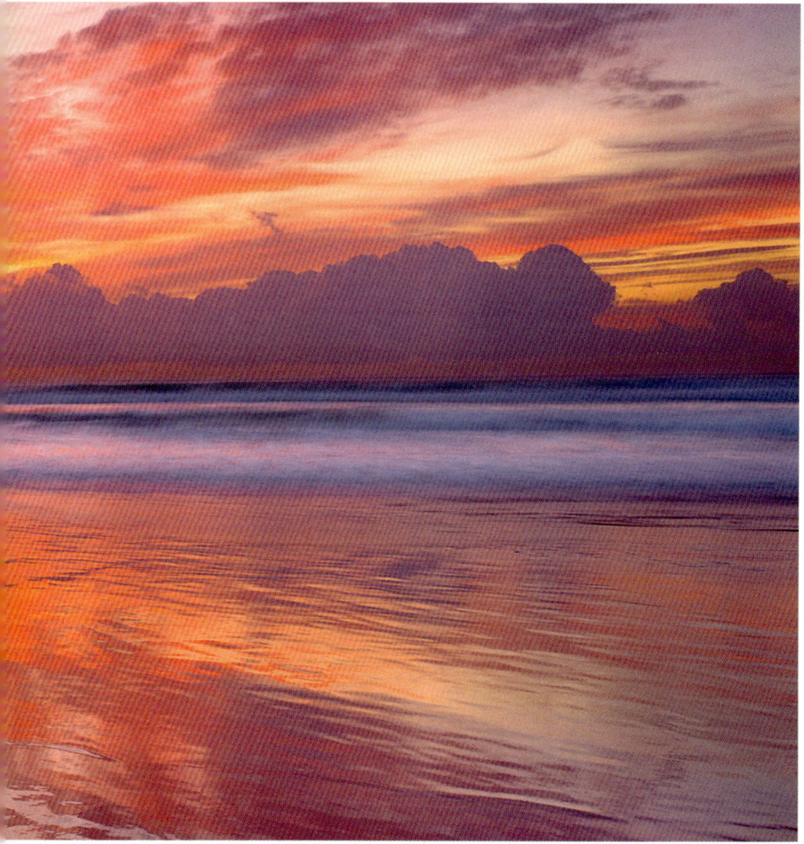

A well-spent day brings happy sleep.

THIS PAGE
Pastel Sunrise, Freshwater Beach, NSW

FOLLOWING PAGES
Mill Stream Falls, Qld

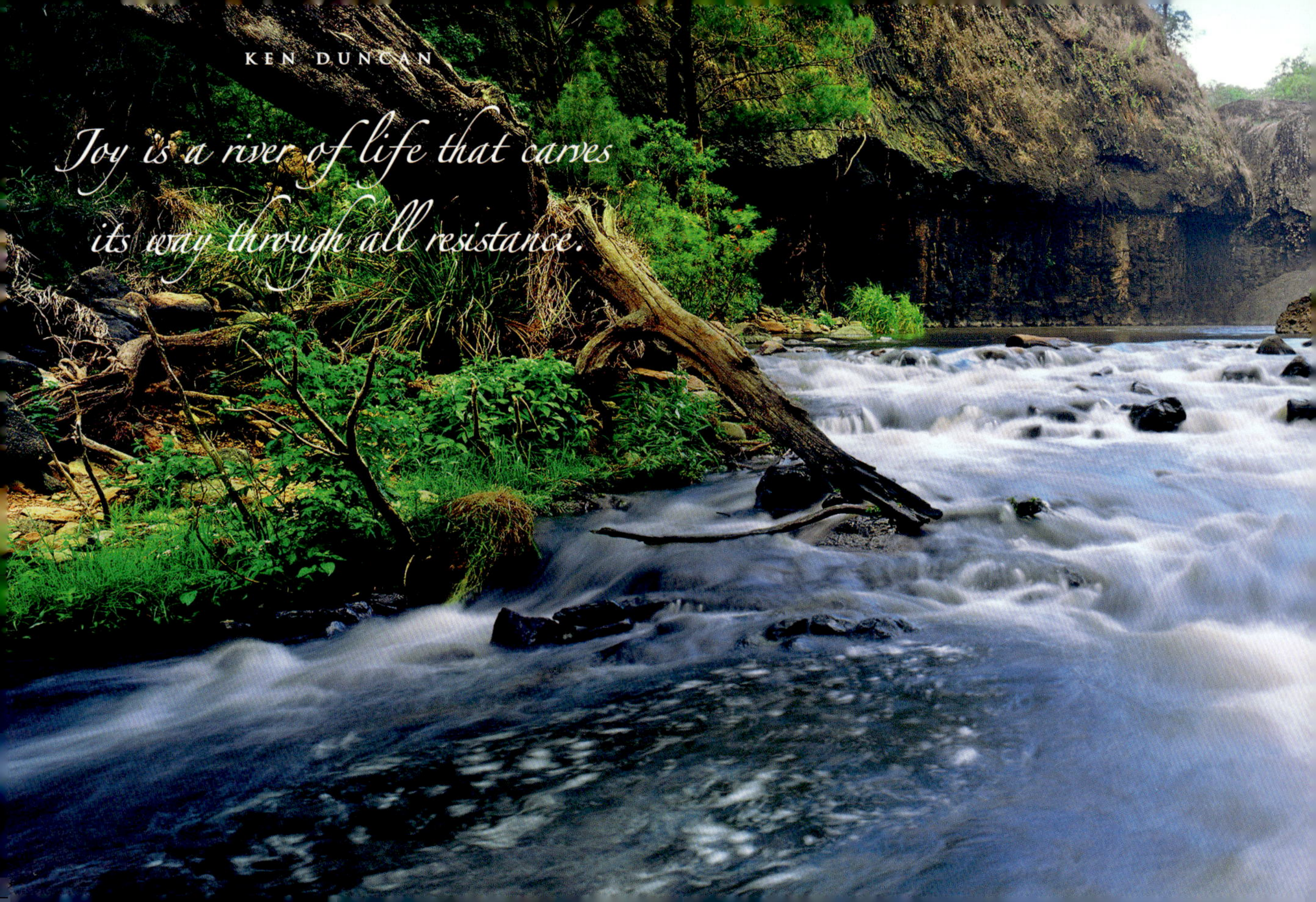

Joy is a river of life that carves its way through all resistance.

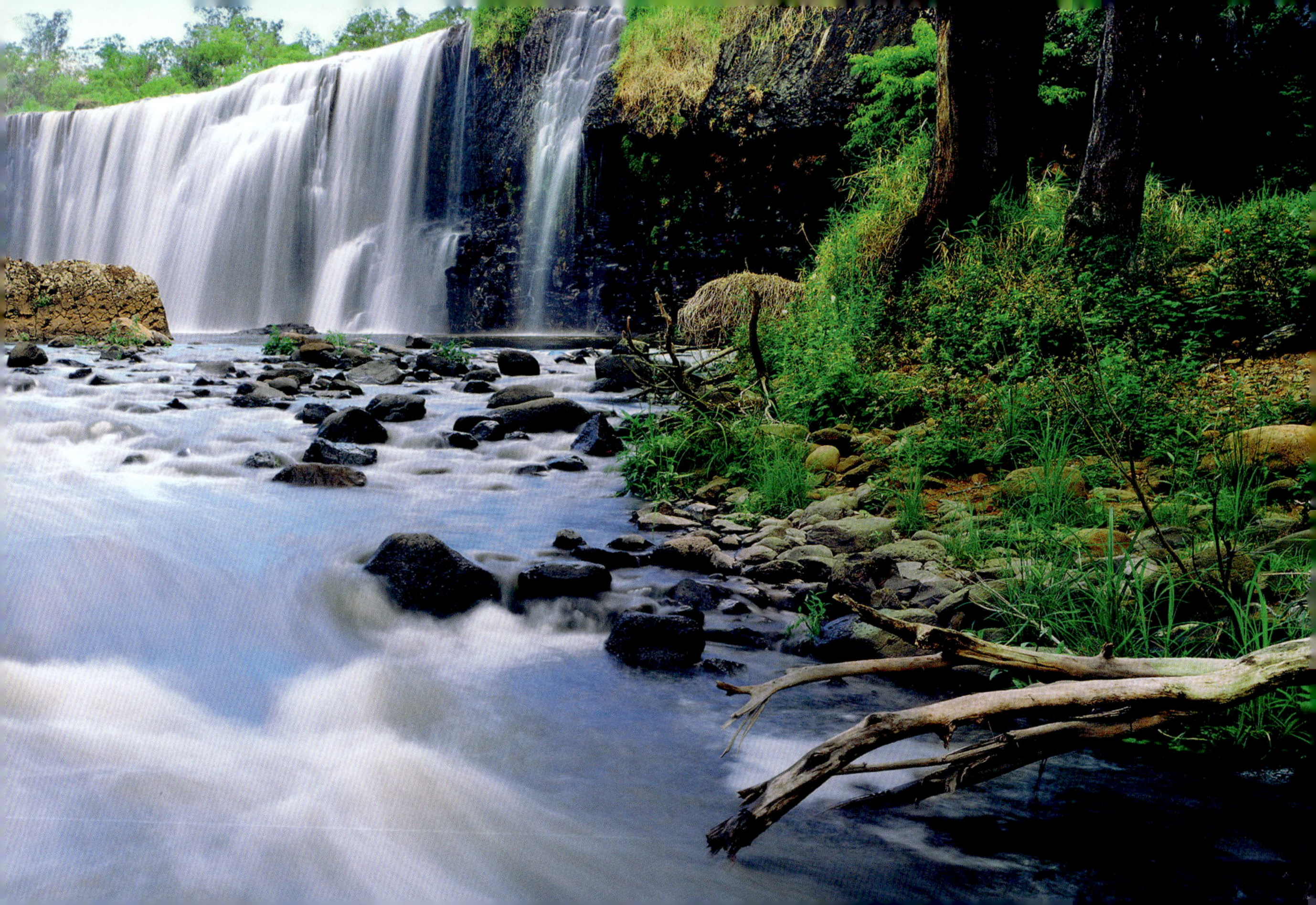

Laughter is the sun that drives winter from the human face.

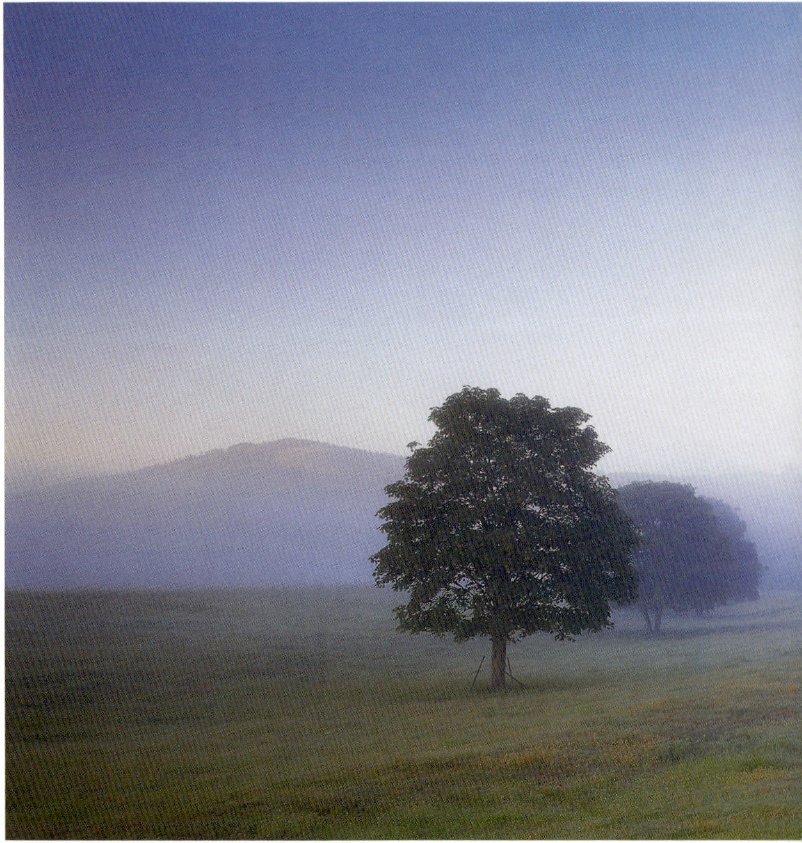

Valley Mist, Omeo, Vic

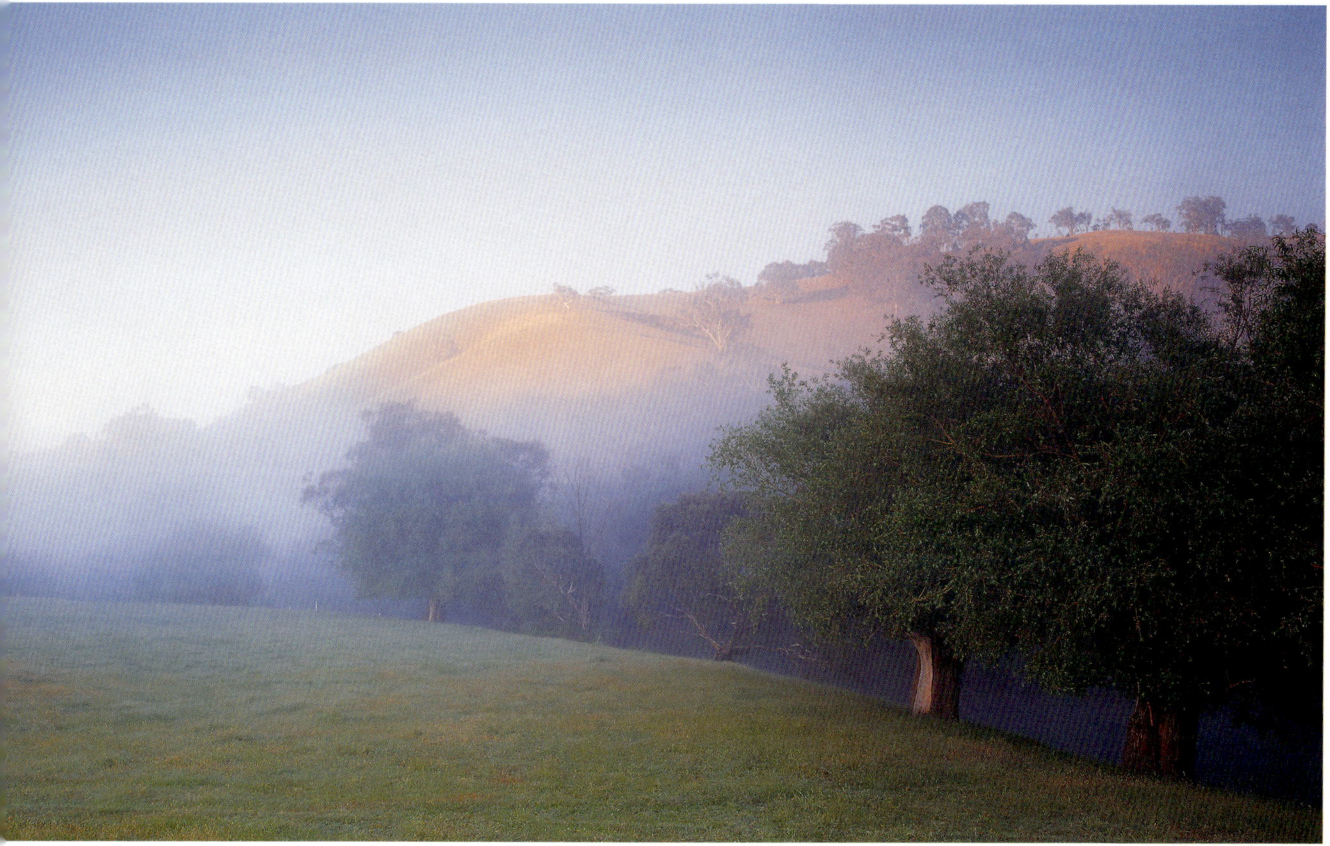

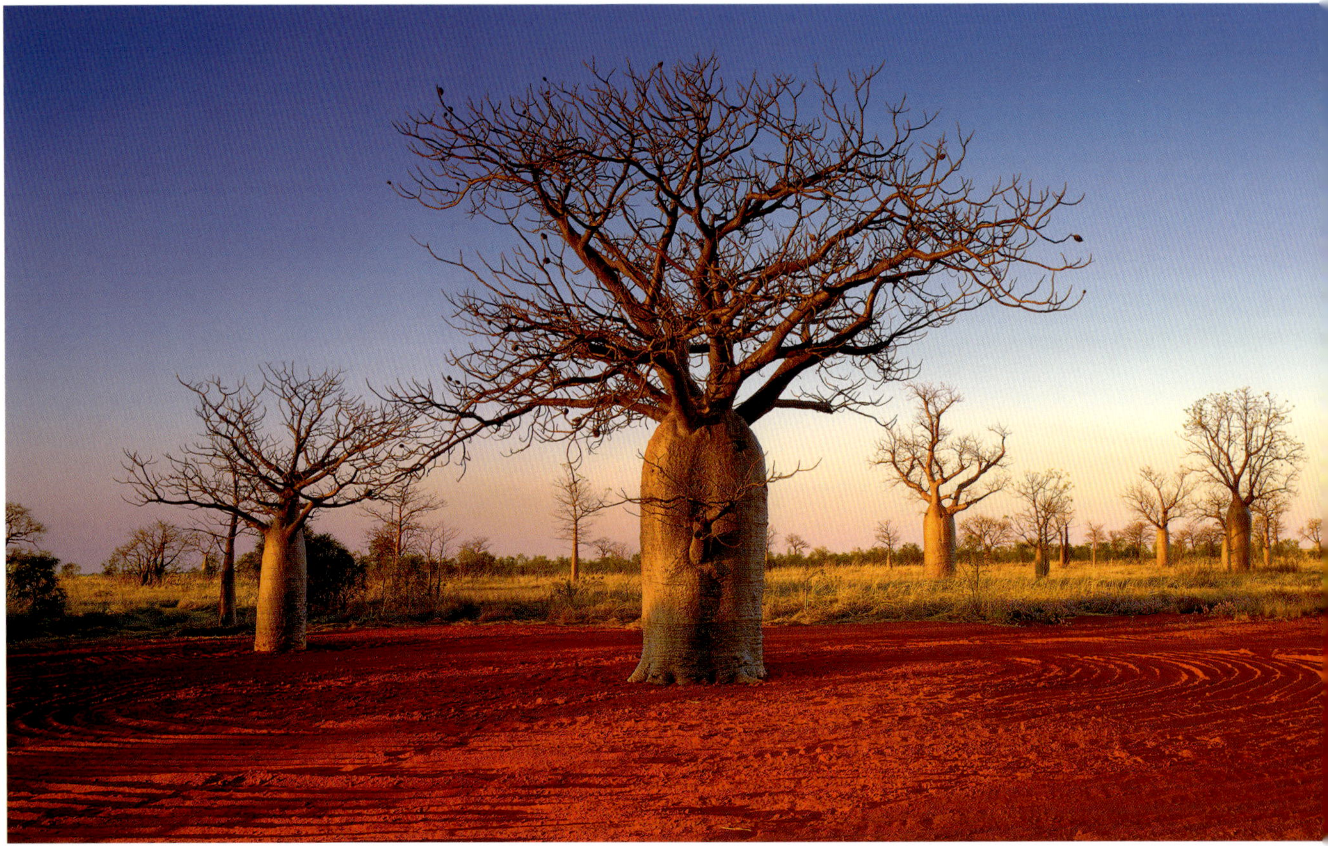

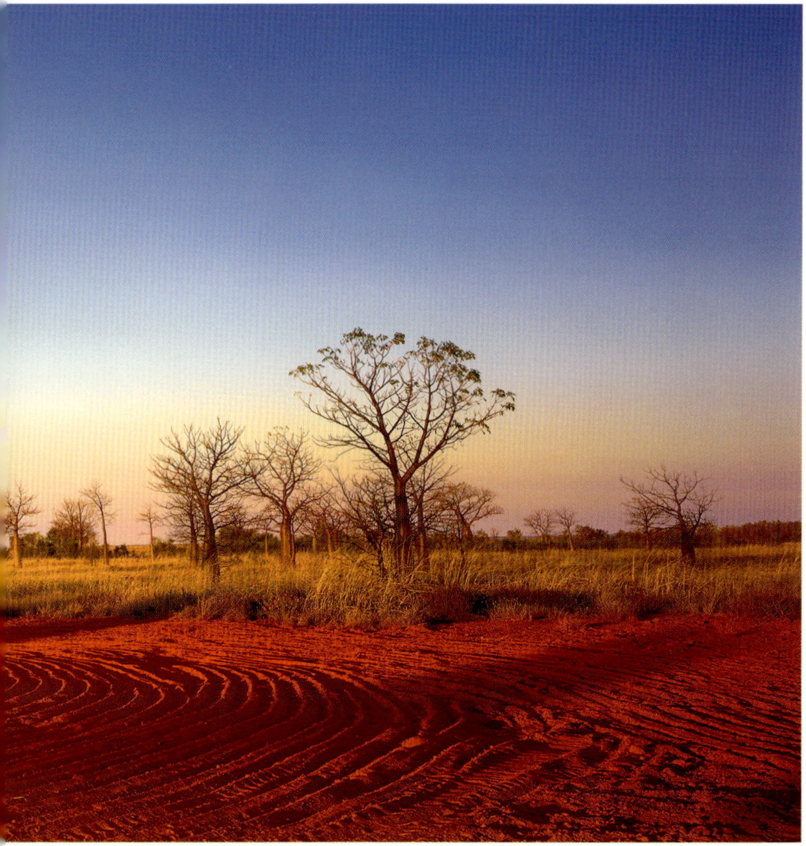

Be joyful in hope,
patient in affliction,
faithful in prayer.

Kimberley Boabs, Derby, WA

ENGLISH PROVERB

A joy that's shared is a joy made double.

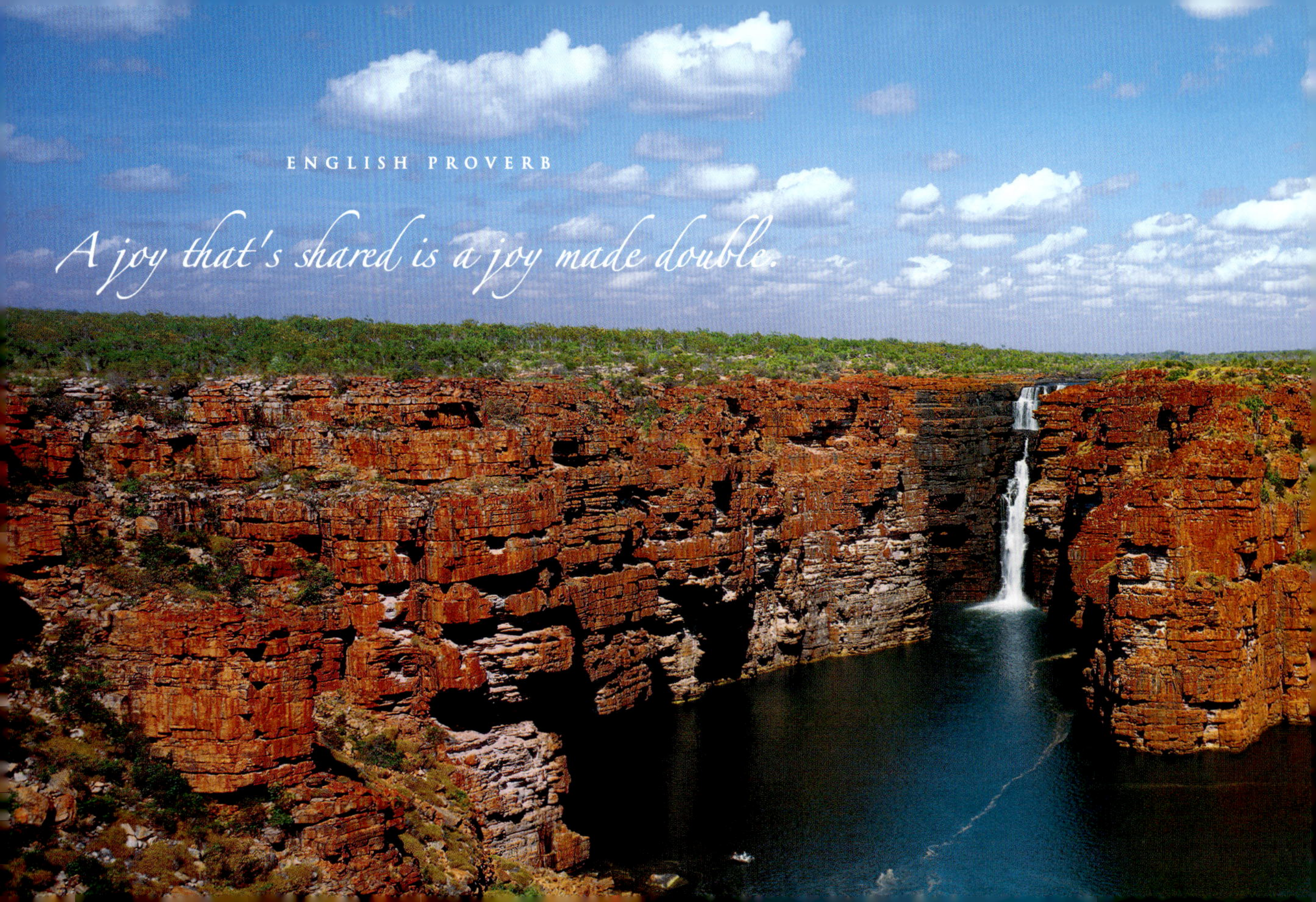

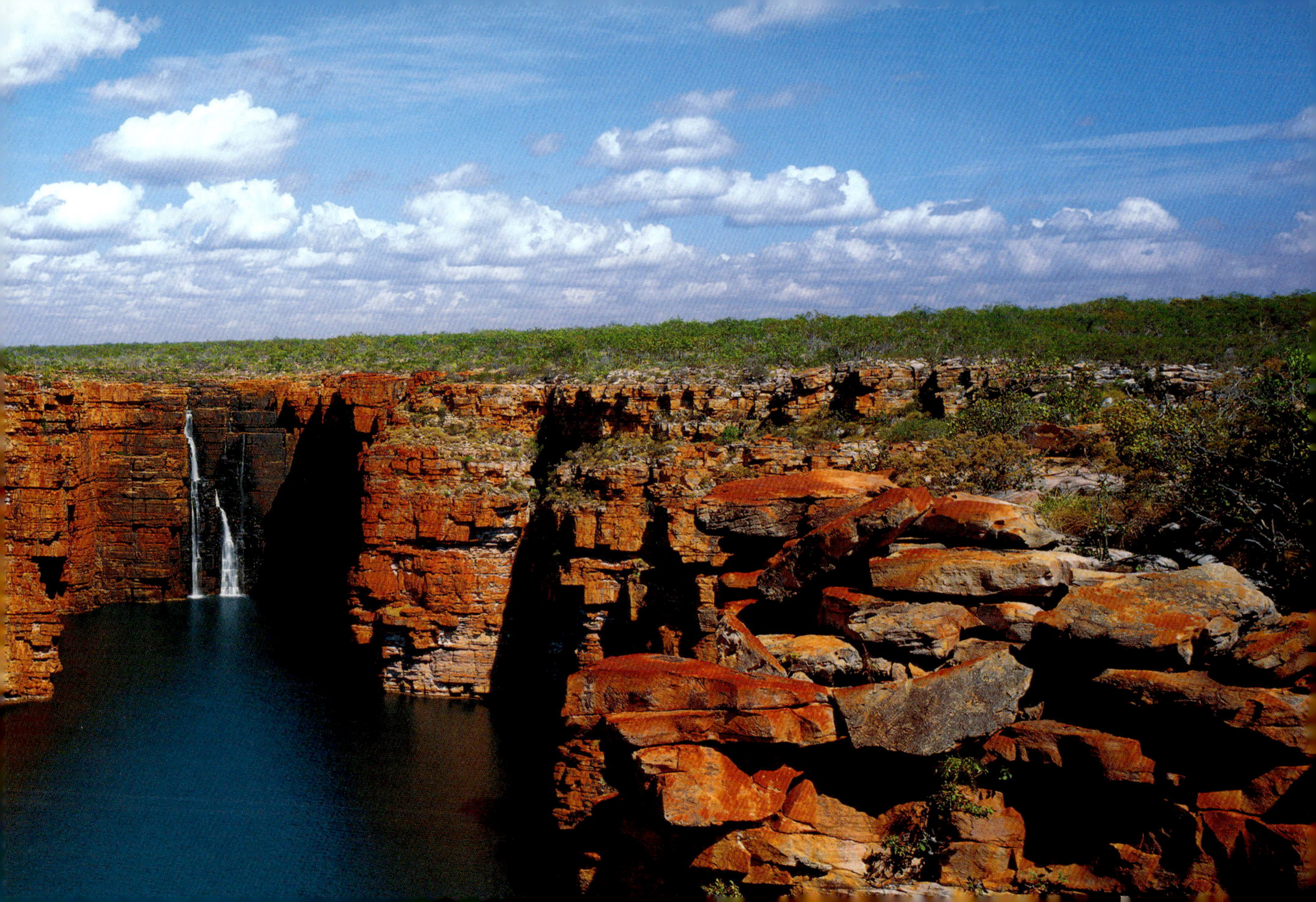

BERNARD MELTZER

Happiness is like a kiss.
You must share it to enjoy it.

PREVIOUS PAGES
Sheer Majesty, The Kimberley, WA

THIS PAGE
Drifting Along, Kakadu, NT

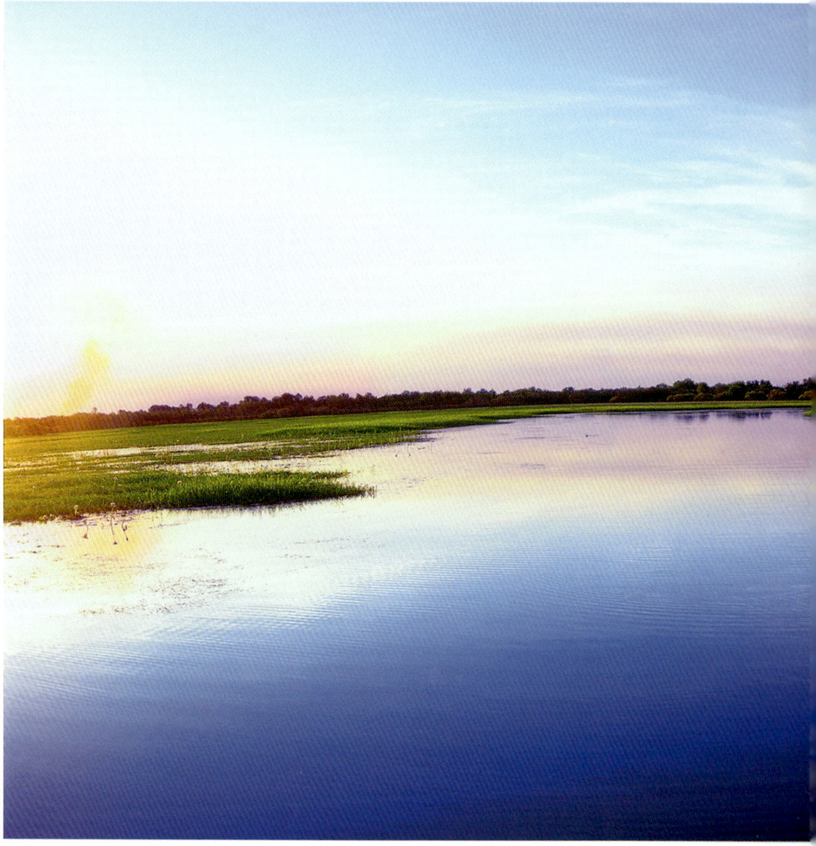

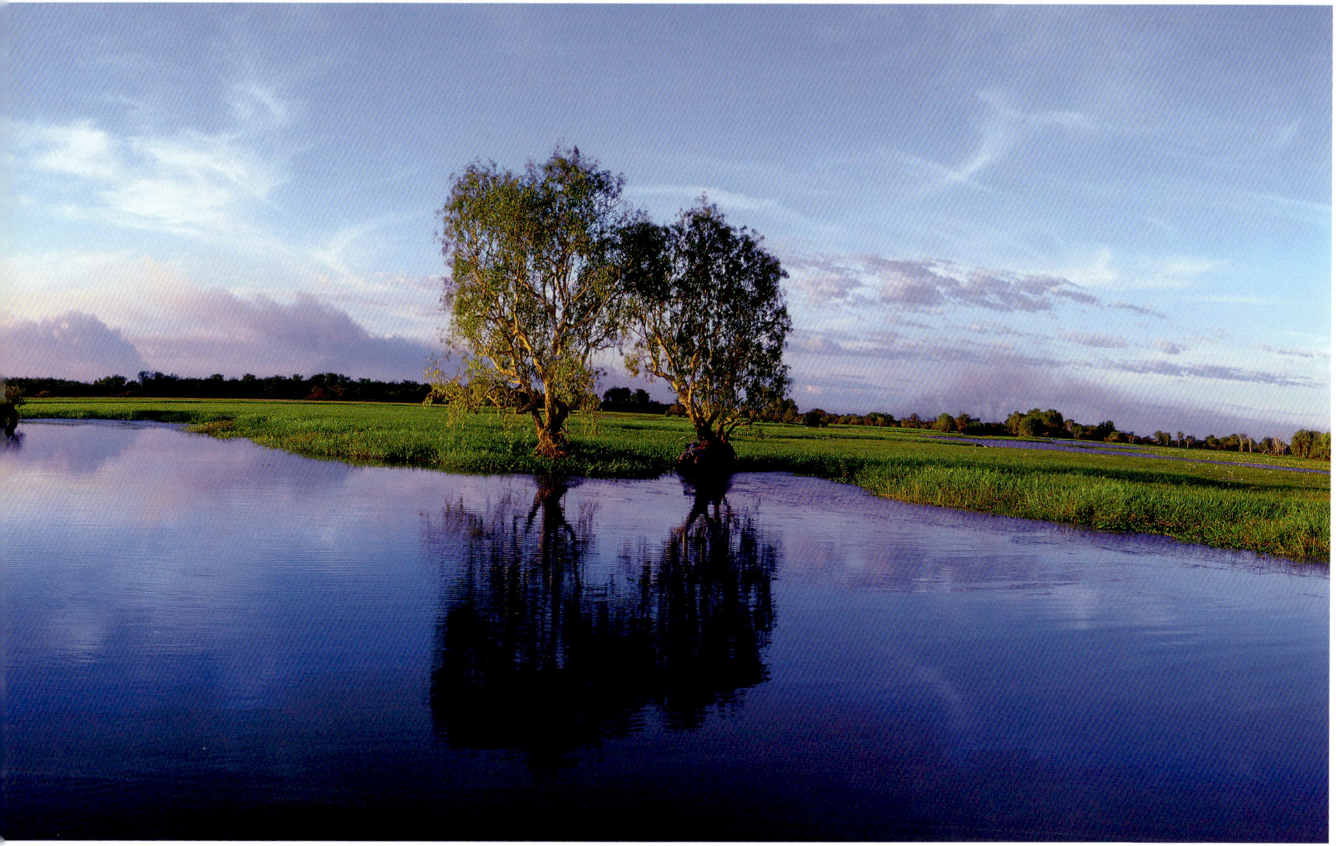

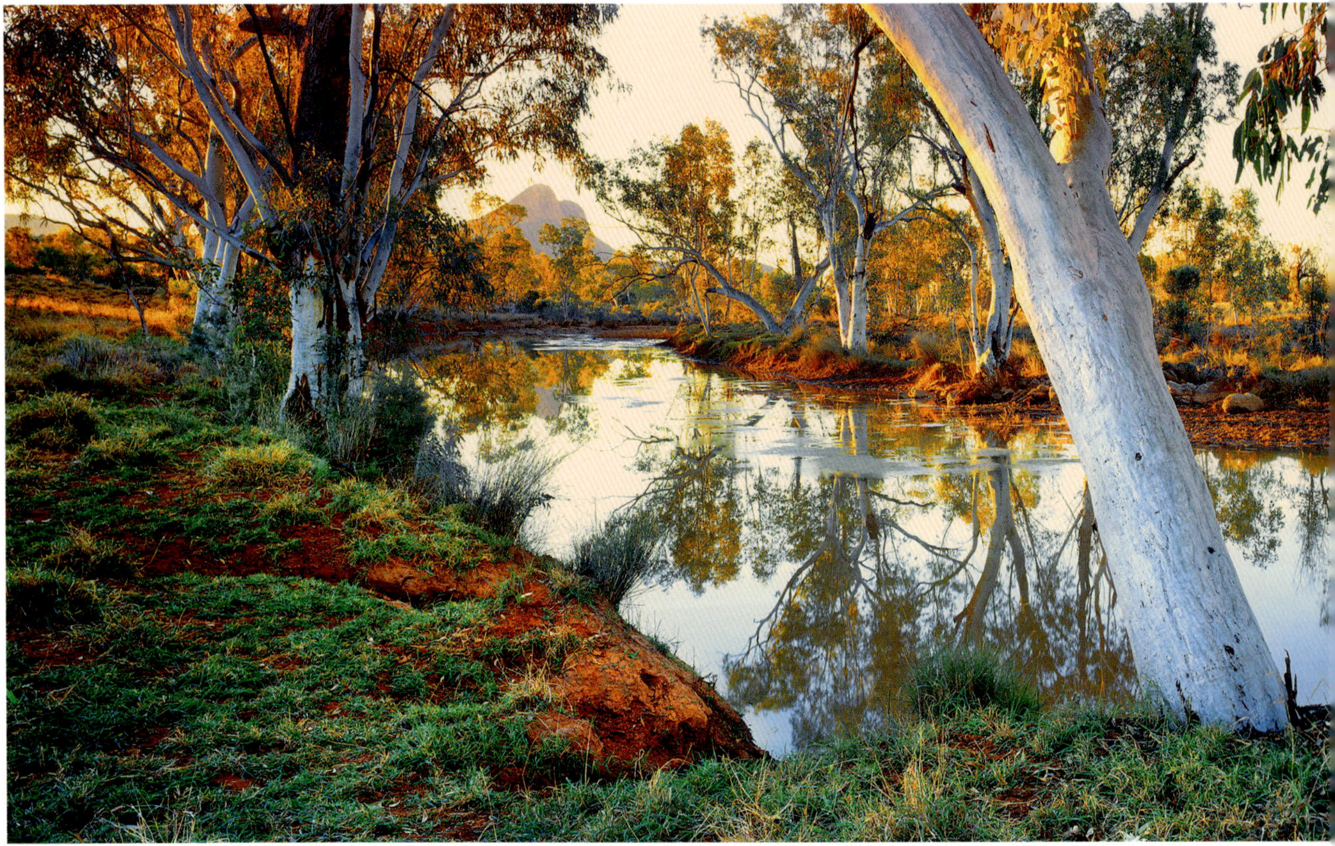

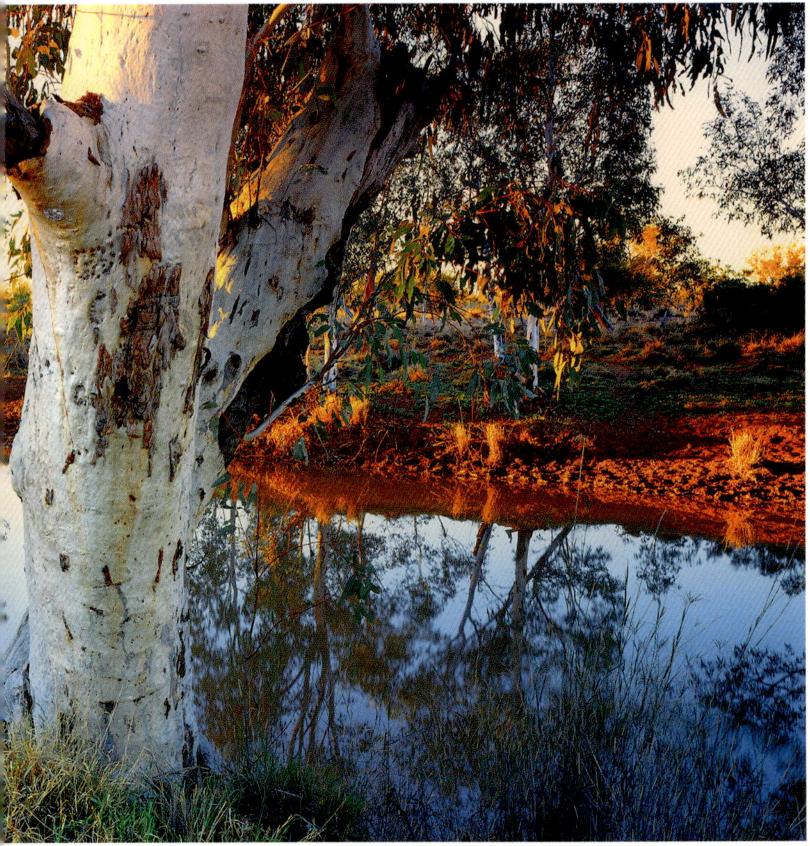

PSALM 28:6-7

Praise be to the Lord,
for he has heard my cry for mercy.
The Lord is my strength and my shield;
my heart trusts in him, and he helps me.
My heart leaps for joy,
and with my song I praise him.

THIS PAGE
Outback Oasis, Junction Waterhole, NT

FOLLOWING PAGES
Arkaba Woolshed, Flinders Ranges, SA

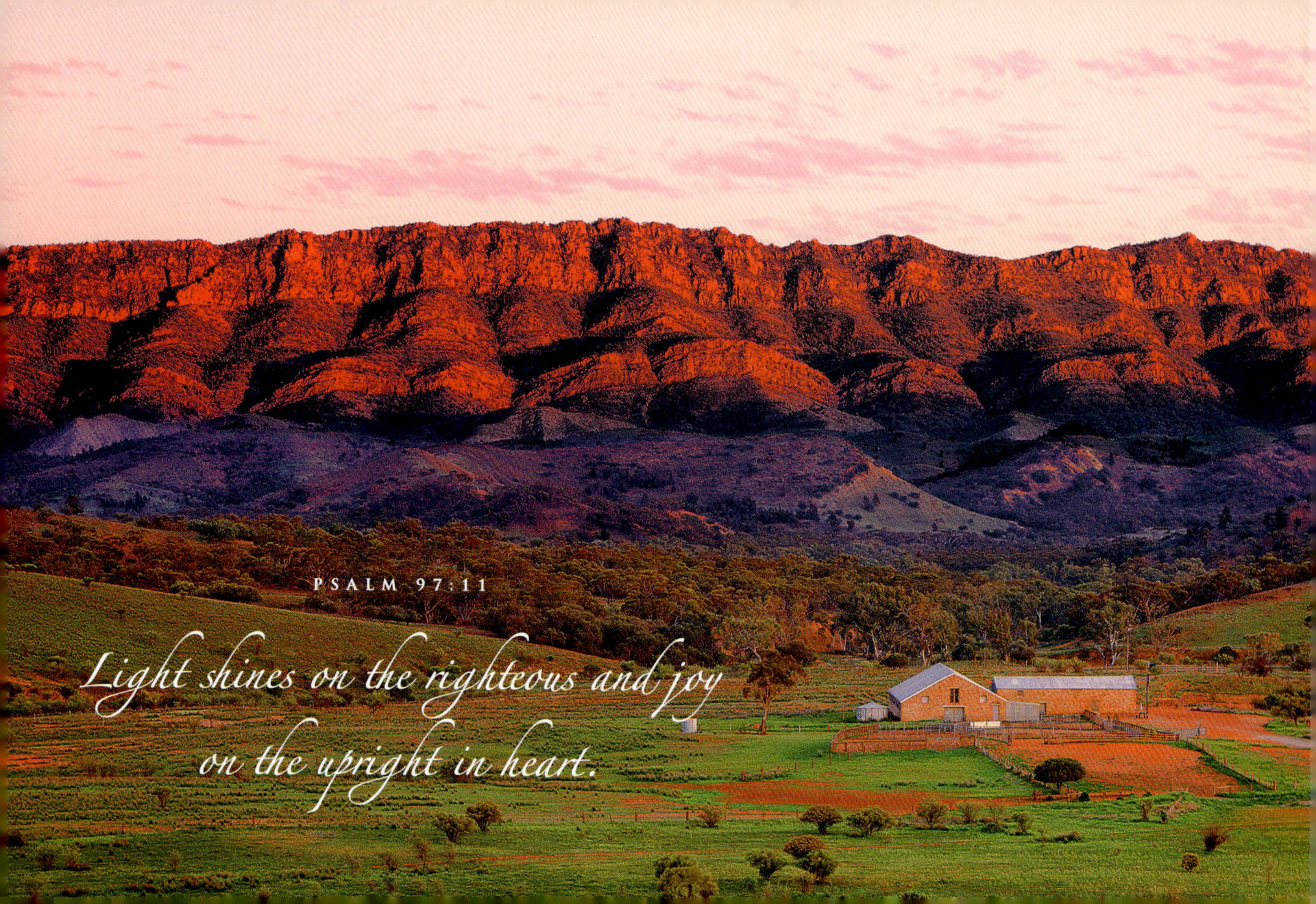
PSALM 97:11
Light shines on the righteous and joy
on the upright in heart.

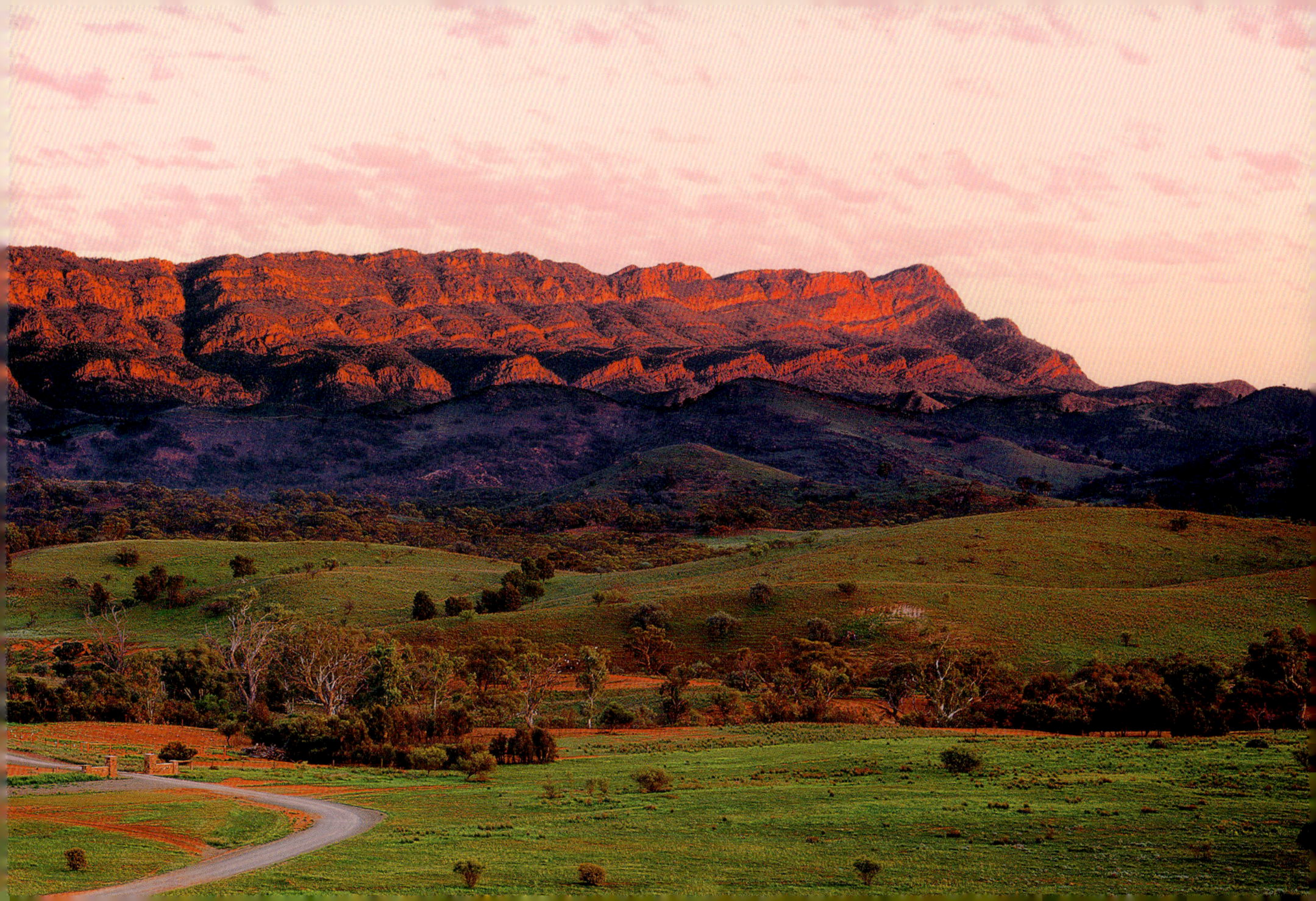

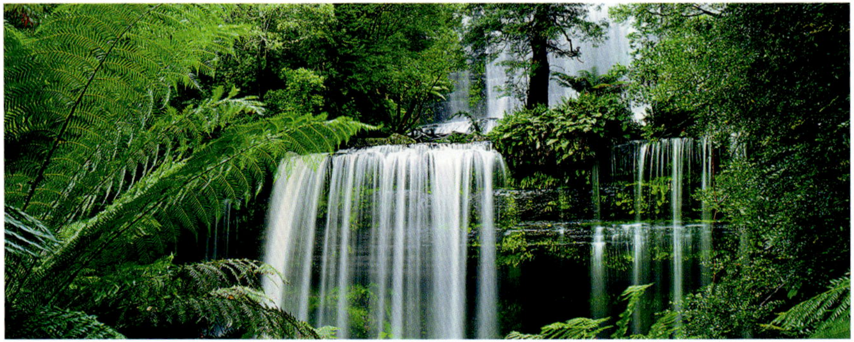

Gift of Life, Russell Falls, Tas

INSPIRATIONAL JOY
First published 2012, Reprinted 2020
by Panographs Publishing Pty Ltd
ABN 21 050 235 606
PO Box 3015 Wamberal
NSW 2260 Australia
Telephone +61 2 4367 6777
Email: exec@kenduncan.com

Photography & text by Ken Duncan
©2020 Divine Guidance P/L
Layout by CFL Print Studio
Reprographics by CFL Print Studio

Printed and bound in China

The National Library of Australia Cataloguing-in-Publication entry
Author: Duncan, Ken
Title: Inspirational joy: Australian photographs / by Ken Duncan
ISBN: 9780987295835 (hbk)

Series: Inspirational books

Subjects:
Photography, Panoramic–Australia
Landscape photography–Australia
Joy–Quotations, maxims, etc
Australia–Pictorial works

Dewey Number: 778.360994

To view the range of Ken Duncan's Limited Edition Prints visit our Gallery:

414 The Entrance Road,
Erina Heights, NSW
Telephone +61 2 4367 6701
Email: erina@kenduncan.com

Or shop online:
www.kenduncan.com